Cambridge Elements ≡

Elements in Complexity and Agent-Based Economics
edited by
Giovanni Dosi
Sant'Anna School of Advanced Studies
Mauro Gallegati
Università Politecnica delle Marche, Ancona
Simone Landini
IRES Piemonte, Torino
Maria Enrica Virgillito
Sant'Anna School of Advanced Studies

AGENT-BASED MODELLING

A Tool for Complexity

Mauro Gallegati
Università Politecnica delle Marche, Ancona

Simone Landini
IRES Piemonte, Torino

Giacomo Gallegati
Università degli Studi di Torino, Collegio Carlo Alberto, Torino, and Université Paris 1 Panthéon-Sorbonne, Paris

CAMBRIDGE
UNIVERSITY PRESS

Shaftesbury Road, Cambridge CB2 8EA, United Kingdom

One Liberty Plaza, 20th Floor, New York, NY 10006, USA

477 Williamstown Road, Port Melbourne, VIC 3207, Australia

314–321, 3rd Floor, Plot 3, Splendor Forum, Jasola District Centre,
New Delhi – 110025, India

103 Penang Road, #05–06/07, Visioncrest Commercial, Singapore 238467

Cambridge University Press is part of Cambridge University Press & Assessment,
a department of the University of Cambridge.

We share the University's mission to contribute to society through the pursuit of
education, learning and research at the highest international levels of excellence.

www.cambridge.org
Information on this title: www.cambridge.org/9781009547635

DOI: 10.1017/9781009547628

First published 2024

A catalogue record for this publication is available from the British Library.

ISBN 978-1-009-54763-5 Hardback
ISBN 978-1-009-54761-1 Paperback
ISSN 2732-5067 (online)
ISSN 2732-5059 (print)

Agent-Based Modelling

A Tool for Complexity

Elements in Complexity and Agent-Based Economics

DOI: 10.1017/9781009547628
First published online: November 2024

Mauro Gallegati
Università Politecnica delle Marche, Ancona

Simone Landini
IRES Piemonte, Torino

Giacomo Gallegati
*Università degli Studi di Torino, Collegio Carlo Alberto, Torino,
and Université Paris 1 Panthéon-Sorbonne, Paris*

Author for correspondence: Simone Landini, landini@ires.piemonte.it

Abstract: This Element works as non-technical overview of Agent-Based Modelling (ABM), a methodology which can be applied to economics, as well as fields of natural and social sciences. This Element presents the introductory notions and historical background of ABM, as well as a general overview of the tools and characteristics of this kind of models, with particular focus on more advanced topics like validation and sensitivity analysis. Agent-based simulations are an increasingly popular methodology which fits well with the purpose of studying problems of computational complexity in systems populated by heterogeneous interacting agents.

Keywords: agent, networks, simulation platforms, validation, sensitivity analysis

JEL classifications: C15, C52, C63, D85, E17, E27, E37, E47, F17, F47, G17, H30, L14

ISBNs: 9781009547635 (HB), 9781009547611 (PB), 9781009547628 (OC)
ISSNs: 2732-5067 (online), 2732-5059 (print)

Contents

Introduction

This Element is about Agent-Based Modelling (ABM) as a tool for the analysis of socioeconomic complex systems. In this respect it can be considered as the 'natural twin' of Landini et al. (2024) about complexity in economics.

The main aim of this Element is to introduce students and scholars to the ABM world, which is a growing stream of research with many applications in different fields within the natural and the social sciences. After reading this Element, the reader will not be able to specify a model based on agents but will have a synthetic and overall view of the main notions and topics of ABM, and how and why they are related to complex systems analysis.

One main point of this Element is to be an accessible guide to taking the first steps in the field. Starting from the main notions and with some historical background, without technicalities, the main tools of ABM, general characteristics, and practices are discussed. A second point is to provide a rich and up-to-date collection of references for further developments: students will largely benefit from the references.

Working with ABM requires modelling, either formal or computational, and computer programming skills. Not only that, but as in any kind of modelling activity, it also requires abstraction capabilities without transforming the research problem into a mathematical or computing problem, that is, without falling into the formalist-computational trap into which mainstream economics has fallen (Landini et al., 2020). Differently said, even though a model based on agents consists of an artificial simulation of a real phenomenon, the goal is reaching a deeper knowledge of facts, especially when these cannot be studied with repeated experiments for events that cannot be replicated. To this end, formalistic abstraction is useful for simplification, neglecting details that can be considered in a second step, without losing touch with reality. In ABM one studies a 'behavioural phenomenology' observable in the real world, to construct virtual agents that simulate the behaviour of real agents by means of appropriate algorithms.

Agent-based models are particularly suited for the study of complex systems because they allow one to managing agents' that realise network formation and interaction.

Nevertheless, there are lights and shadows. Although the ABM approach is promising, there are elements of concern. Agent-Based Modelling still lacks a sufficiently structured theory, since it is at a level of maturity not yet comparable with that of the mainstream, at least to the extent of considering ABM not just an approach or a technique but a discipline as well as econometrics that can be applied in almost every field of science. In ABM there is no shortage of methods of implementation, results, solutions, developments and contributions in a wide spectrum of research fields, and they are still growing, but this happens without 'coordination'. Also, the present Element will be useful for novices, who will appreciate a survey of application platforms.

Section 1 is devoted to modelling through ABM methodology. Agent-Based Modelling is an indispensable tool to be able to analyse complex systems, as well as a laboratory for the economist, dealing with the construction of ABM models, their theoretical conditions, and their empirical validity. We first introduce the notion of agent in Section 1.1. Section 1.2 considers heterogeneity and network interaction, which can be understood as the main determinants of complexity one can easily manage with ABM simulation. After having introduced these fundamental aspects, Section 1.3 introduces a short description of ABM as a methodology for modelling and Section 1.4 offers a short history of the method. Section 2 is concerned with tools and notions of ABM. In Section 2.1 we introduce notions about the tools in ABM simulation such as the mostly diffused platforms, and in Section 2.2 a guide to the literature about ABM tools is discussed. All the previous elements prepare the field for Section 2.3 that develops the general characteristics of an ABM before passing to the fundamental aspects of validation and sensitivity analysis in Sections 2.4 and 2.5 respectively. Section 3 concludes the Element.

G.G., M.G., S.L.

1 Agent-Based Modelling

Agent-based models potentially present a way to model the [. . .] economy as a complex system, as Keynes attempted to do, while taking human adaptation and learning into account, as Lucas advocated. Such models allow for the creation of a kind of virtual universe in which many players can act in complex – and realistic – ways.

J. Doyne Farmer and Duncan Foley, '*The economy needs agent-based modelling*'.

Agent-Based Modelling is a computational approach for the study of systems with heterogeneous and interacting agents. The behavioural rules of artificial agents are simpler than those activated by the real agents; as can be observed from the composition of their micro-behaviours, these systems follow emergent dynamics that we would not have been able to understand just by considering the behaviour of the individuals. By aggregating the results we can make inferences about system-level regularities, and we can explain why some are more persistent than others. This has two implications: (i) empirical regularities (not universal laws) are a priori unknown, and (ii) they are not attributable to individual behaviour but are proper to the hierarchies of the system. In almost all ABMS we find one or more species of agents with characteristic properties, both related to their endowments and to their ways of acting and interacting, very often only in a local network. Moreover, artificial agents have the possibility of changing their behaviours by choosing among a set of rules of action, as if trying to adapt to changes in the context.

1.1 The Agent

There is no single definition of 'agent' in the literature. The agents of an ABM (socioeconomic) are decision-making machines that emulate the behaviour of the individuals of the system. They receive information from outside (e.g., from the market or from other agents) that they then manage, store in memory, and process through algorithms emulating the behavioural processes of real agents. As a decision-making machine encoded in a computer program, the agent of an ABM is subject to the efficiency of the software and the power of the hardware and is 'built' by the programmer who decodes the capacity of action in an artificial world.

To the best of our knowledge, Holland and Miller (1991) were the first to introduce the term 'agent': 'An agent in such a [complex adaptive] system is adaptive if it satisfies an additional pair of criteria: the actions of the agent in its environment can be assigned a value (performance, utility, payoff, fitness, or the like); and the agent behaves so as to increase this value over time.' Tesfatsion (2021) claims:

> The term Agent-Based Modeling refers to a class of modelling approaches designed for the study of systems whose dynamics are driven by successive interactions among heterogeneous entities. Such systems range from the particle systems studied in physics to the coupled human and natural systems studied in socioecology. [Agents are conceived] in broad terms, as software entities able to represent individuals, social groupings, institutions, biological entities, and/or physical entities. ... Given initial modeler-specified agent states, all world events arise entirely from agent interactions. (Box 1)

In general, an agent is any entity capable of acting, namely, of performing sophisticated actions, from the mere reaction to some stimulus up to the highest level of proactivity. The spectrum of possibilities is very wide, as is the range of entities that perform actions.

As the agents of the real world are heterogeneous, so also are those of the artificial world of an ABM. Heterogeneity can be defined in at least two ways. On the one hand, we can consider 'structural' heterogeneity, which concerns the internal state of the agent's equipment, and on the other, 'behavioural' heterogeneity, which concerns the way of action. This last aspect brings us to the topic of interaction with other agents or the environment, in both direct and indirect ways.

Box 1 The c-ABM theoretical framework of Tesfatsion (2021).

Agent-Based Modelling is a class of modelling approaches for the study of systems whose dynamics are determined by repeated interactions among heterogeneous agents. Agent-based Computational Economics (ACE) is a variant of ABM, identified by Tesfatsion in 1996, in which the agent is understood as active software in an artificially constructed world, acting as a function of its state – described by data, properties, and methods or functions – by which individual and collective entities are represented, from whose interaction the events of the artificial world are generated. Tesfatsion (2021) proposes the c-ABM variant, where 'c' means 'complete' because it is based on seven fundamental principles that (i) describe a computationally based general approach, from which logical rigour is derived, and (ii) allow a high degree of flexibility. The c-ABM principles are 'methodological axioms' for defining a core set of arguments on which to develop a general theory of ABM.

The first six principles concern the characterisation of a system described by a model, in 'initial-value state-space form'. This model evolves in the successive iterations of a computer execution, indexing the various events along a schedule that starts from an 'initial instant' and ends at a 'final deadline', and that fulfils given boundary conditions, established as constraints, specified to determine the initial condition.

The first principle concerns the definition of an agent as a software, an abstraction of a real entity, which lives in an artificially constructed world and whose ability to act depends on its state (data) and methods (functions). The second principle concerns entities, individual or collective, that are representable with the generic notion of an agent. The third principle concerns local constructiveness, understood as the ability of an agent to act at each instant by means of a function of its state at each iteration. The fourth principle concerns the autonomy of the agent, which acts without any coordination from outside but, at most, under the restrictions that characterise it by qualifying its behaviour. The fifth principle concerns the constructiveness of the system, that is, the fact that the state of a computationally constructed system depends only on the set of actions of its constituents at each iteration. The sixth principle concerns the historicity of the system, that is the fact that, once the initial conditions are fixed, the changes of state of the agents and of the system are determined by the events that are realised through the interactions among the agents. The seventh principle is completely different from the others because it places limits on the researchers, who must limit themself to specifying the initial configuration, leaving the system to evolve to analyse the results without intervening with an observation that could disturb the evolution of the system.

Based on these founding principles, an ABM becomes a computational laboratory for exploring an artificially constructed world. If the model refers to a real system or phenomenon, then it is through the c-ABM that a computational simulation paradigm can be introduced. An approach that is as flexible as it is logically rigorous for simulating the 'world as it is', obviously accepting some simplifications depending on the purpose, rather than the computational reduction of the 'world as we would like it to be' or the representation of a conceptual experiment by a 'toy model'. Based on the flexibility and logical rigor of c-ABM, the computational method of simulation can be said to be the 'mathematics for the analysis of the real world' in a realistic way, not just verisimilitude, which surpasses the traditional formalistic modelling in a way that is closer to the 'reasoning of mathematics', that is to say, detached from the real world it wants to describe.

As we will see, it is through interaction that the agent becomes a 'social' entity open to the outside world. Moreover, as the economic agent can behave as it considers more opportune in relation to its own rules of behaviour, that is, it is free to follow its own will, so also the artificial agent of an ABM can be constructed in such a way as to be able to choose how to behave when the context changes.[1]

The agent is therefore capable of *adapting* to the changing state of its environment and *learning* from its own or others' experience. To be able to learn, the agent must have *memory* and *sociality*. Sociality means that the agents make a community and interact, sometimes competitively, and exchange information and can change their behavioural rules.

The analogy between the notion of an agent and the human individual obviously is incomplete. Among many other features overlooked here, it is worth mentioning that some properties are exclusively human, and therefore (almost) impossible to be trained in an agent of a model; for example, the human capacity of abstract thinking, of posing new problems in an autonomous way, and of feeling and emotions. The human being is certainly rational, but rationality does not consist in finding the optimal solution according to some calculation scheme. Rationality is reasonableness, that is the ability to do the best we can, even while giving up the theoretical optimum. The information available

---

[1] In agent simulation, it is possible to construct agents who conceal important information from others, attempt to extract confidential information from others, or mislead them to act to their advantage. The so-called belief-desire-intention (BDI) scheme, inspired by Bratman's (1987) theory of practical reasoning, allows us to describe the mechanism by which the agent separates the planning phase of its actions from the implementation, and allows us also to treat agents with limited rationality.

is not only limited and unequally distributed, but each agent is endowed with bounded rationality.[2] The fact that an entity is endowed with limited rationality means that its decision-making capabilities are limited even in the presence of full information. It is with these resources that the agent faces any decision-making problem. Consequently, the optimality of the solution to the agent's decision problem can at most be posed in terms of a relative or local optimum, not an absolute or global optimum.

The arguments discussed so far sketch the notion of an agent based on a 'behavioural phenomenology' observable in the real world. With these characteristics in mind, we now consider how we can construct a virtual agent that simulates a real agent. Initially, we can design the agent as an algorithm. An agent of an ABM model is a software that considers at least two of the discussed features: structural heterogeneity, which refers to the variables (or data) that describe its internal state and endowments, and behavioural heterogeneity, which refers to the decision and behaviour rules (or functions), and thus also refers to the interaction with the outside world.

1.2 Interaction, Networks, and Heterogeneity

Interaction is a particular type of action that occurs between at least two entities. For an interaction to be realised, it is necessary that at least one of the two entities is equipped with an interface with which to recognise its counterpart to communicate information, understood in the most general sense proposed by Rosen (1986): 'In human terms, information is easy to define: it is anything that is or can be answered to a question' (p. 3). Starting from this simple definition we can identify at least two categories of interaction, the *direct* and the *indirect* one.[3]

Interaction is direct when the interfaces of two individual interacting entities allow 'one-to-one' reciprocal action, that is, when one counterpart can communicate a request to the other and the latter is able to communicate its

---

[2] The notion of 'bounded rationality' is attributed to Herbert Simon (1957).

[3] In terms of direct interaction, this can be *local*, if everyone communicates only with a small group of counterparts, or *global*, if everyone communicates with everyone in the system. Local or global, depending on the purpose, direct interaction can be *voluntary* – the individual chooses his counterparts – or *induced* – the individual has no choice but to communicate only with given counterparts. If the association between counterparts is governed by choice criteria, typically based on expectations about the successful outcome of their encounter, the *interaction* is said to be *stochastic*, that is, the interaction is interpretable as an event. The simplest, and most particular, case of stochastic interaction is when individuals meet by chance, which is tractable with a random communication framework (Kirman, 1983) or with 'random matching' procedures (Ioannides, 1990; Bak et al., 1996). If the interacting individuals do not choose their counterparts, nor do they meet them randomly, then the interaction is induced and thus we speak of *deterministic interaction*, that is, conveyed by a predetermined relational infrastructure.

response to the former. In all this what matters is that one speaks to the other and that the speech is exclusive to each other, not to multiple different entities.

Interaction is an event, situated in space and time, that occurs as a reciprocal action between entities enabled to communicate by their interfaces. The spatio-temporal situation concerns the historicity of their relationships. That is, the two agents may already be related for reasons other than those for which they now interact, or it is precisely for interacting that they now establish a new relationship. In fact, at the basis of interaction there is 'sociality', namely, connectivity (Casti, 1979) understood as belonging to a network structure (also multi-level) in which the nodes represent the agents and the links represent the connections that support the interactions.[4] The network that supports the interaction is a relational infrastructure in which two agents can recognise each other and decide whether to communicate or not. The spatio-temporal situation is therefore defined by a relational infrastructure that can be a network in which the relationships among the nodes already exist, but then the relationships are activated or deactivated in the time, or where the number of nodes varies in the time and, with it, also the valence of the ties.

Each network as relational infrastructure that supports interaction can be associated with a graph, where nodes/agents can be connected by oriented links, that is, with an arrow uniquely oriented from A to B or from B to A, or by simple links, that is, with a segment doubly oriented from A to B and also from B to A. In the first case the matrix that represents the connections is said to be of incidence, and in the second case the matrix that represents the connections is said to be of adjacency: the last one is necessarily symmetrical, while the other may not be. In both cases, the existence of the relationship can be indicated with the value 1, while 0 indicates the absence of the relationship. That is, if, at the intersection of the row of node A and the column of node B, 1 is written, then A and B interact, and vice versa. Sometimes, instead of binary values, you can use 'weighted' values that express the intensity of the relationships and are represented on the graph with more or less marked traits depending on the intensity. A network as a relational infrastructure can change in time – both with respect to the links that turn on (1) or turn off (0) and with respect to the number of nodes that compose the oriented or simple graph – depending on the state and behaviour of the agents.

Indirect interaction also admits a graphical representation. For example, firms and consumers can be indirectly related by the fact of being customers of the same bank, even if none of the consumers either works for any of these firms or is in any way a customer of it: what agglomerates these agents into a network, typically star-shaped, is only the fact of being customers of a bank. A bit more sophisticated

---

[4] For an introduction to network theory and practice see, among others, Wasserman and Faust (2008), Scott and Carrington (2011), Caldarelli and Catanzaro (2012), and Knoke and Yang (2019).

and factually real is the following example. Suppose that the members a group of consumers are all customers of bank A (A-consumers) and a group of firms are all customers of bank B (B-firms), and that A and B in turn interact in the interbank market. The A-consumers and the B-firms are related and interact indirectly to the extent that the behaviours of the A-consumers and the B-firms change the type of relationship between A and B, such that A changes its relationships with its A-consumers and B changes its relationships with its B-firms. In this case the overall graph is composed of two stars connected by a bridge between A and B. The topology is further complicated if some A-consumers are customers of some B-firms and if some B-firms have hired some A-consumers. In this case the stars are melded into one single network that is said to be bipartite.[5] On the first level we place A and B between them, and on the second level we place all A-consumers connecting them to each other and to A and all B-firms connecting them to each other and to B, but then we also draw arcs between the subset C(A|B) of A-consumers buying from B and the subset F(B|A) of B-firms that have hired A-consumers. Also, the bipartite network can change through time.

In fact, a network as a relational infrastructure that supports interactions is an emergent phenomenon of the system, due to the interactive behaviour of agents of various species. Note that a network can also exist between agents of the same type, at most heterogeneous with respect to their endowments – structural heterogeneity – while it is not necessary that they are heterogeneous also with respect to their behaviours – behavioural heterogeneity – or to their species. However, as mentioned earlier, heterogeneity and interaction are coupled categories of complexity (Landini and Gallegati, 2014). If we interact in order to acquire information, as stated earlier according to Rosen (1986), and information is typically asymmetric and incomplete, it is also true that interaction can both contribute to diffuse part of the information but also create new asymmetries, hence a new need to interact and so on. So, in fact, what mainly counts in characterising a system as complex is the interaction that is part of the behavioural heterogeneity of the agents. On the other hand, although animated by the same goal, even if initially homogeneous in their endowments, agents can interact in different ways, for example by cooperating or competing. When we deal with complex human systems, we analyse relational networks. These support the interactive behaviours from which phenomena emerge that are proper to the system, and the same network is a representation of the system and not of the single individuals that compose it. From a complex system emerges a complex network (Reichardt, 2009; Caldarelli, 2010;

---

[5] A bipartite network is a network in which there are at least two disjoint groups of nodes in which some nodes of the first group, which can be among them in relation also for the simple belonging to the group, connect to some nodes of the second group, which can be among them in relation also for the simple belonging to the group. The two groups of nodes can be graphically represented on two levels.

Caldarelli and Chesa, 2016) evolving, changing, and reconfiguring. In conclusion, one way to model interaction is to ground it in the notion of communication between agents and, therefore, to situate it in space and time with networks. In an economic system, social agents are interconnected by many kinds of relationships that determine different networks, and the state of each depends directly or indirectly on that of many others.

An economy is therefore an interactive system of heterogeneous agents. Among the various behaviours of a social agent there is also the interactive one; in fact it is precisely because of its ability to interact that an agent can be called 'social', and this is true both for agents who choose their counterparts and for those who are placed in interaction (Kirman, 1983; Kirman et al., 1986; Kirman, 1999). The heterogeneity of agents with respect to their states, which are also influenced by the states of other agents, and their behaviours, among which the interactive one is the most relevant, make an economy a complex system. Heterogeneity and interaction are not separable but, rather, they are two sides of the same coin, which we call 'sociality', from which the complexity of the system originates (Landini and Gallegati, 2014), in which interactions are conveyed by networks of relationships. That is, identical interacting agents become different (in states and behaviors) and different agents are stimulated to interact. Bookstaber and Kirman (2018; p. 770) explain that, as much as it is not essential for the system to be initially heterogeneous in order to be complex: 'Heterogeneity almost inevitably leads the economy to be a complex adaptive system ... A collection of particles individuals who are, at the outset, identical, may change their state as they interact with other particles and the result will be configurations of particles in different states which will be difficult or even impossible to predict from an analysis of the particles in isolation.' In short, heterogeneity and interaction are 'entangled' categories of complexity because identical interacting agents become different and different agents are induced to interact, that is, interaction generates heterogeneity and heterogeneity leads to interaction.

1.3 What ABM Is About

Agent-based modelling is a computational simulation method that implements a program executable by a computer according to a model, a simplified and somehow formalised representation of 'something' that exists in the real world, based on the agent, that we may initially intend as any entity capable of acting.

The ABM methodology is adopted by many disciplines and the number of contributions that use it is growing rapidly, both because of the increasing diffusion of computers and 'low-cost' programming languages and because simulation is often the only way to study complexity, or those phenomena that cannot be experimentally replicated (in economics as in astronomy or volcanology). Given the modest empirical success of *mainstream* economics, high hopes are placed in ABM (LeBaron and Tesfatsion, 2008; Farmer and Foley, 2009; Borrill and Tesfatsion, 2010; and Bookstaber, 2017). However, despite its growing popularity, at present users of ABM are not yet fully satisfied with its results (Axtell and Farmer, 2023).

Leombruni et al. (2006) propose a set of best practices for doing ABM simulation in socioeconomic disciplines. Their proposal follows from highlighting the main limitations of this approach, at least in its current state of development. In particular, the contribution of these scholars is important because they describe some of the weaknesses of this approach that motivate the traditional modeler to look at ABM with scepticism. A reason for dissatisfaction with the ABM approach, sometimes even on the part of those who adopt it and contribute to its development, and which leaves those who do not adopt it perplexed, is that at present there is no sufficiently structured formal theory so general that ABM can be made a discipline, which can be applied to specify any agent model in any field of research. To put it bluntly, just as econometrics is a discipline that can be applied to any context in which we have cross-sectional and/or time-dependent data, ABM is still far from achieving a similar level of generalisation insofar as it can be applied to a wide range of phenomena in almost any discipline, but this is done in a loosely organised way. Nevertheless, some breakthroughs are being made. For example, North (2014) proposes a 'theoretical formalism for analysing agent-based models', while Tesfatsion (2021) proposes a theorisation (Box 1) starting with the idea of an agent as a 'software entity within a computationally-constructed world, able to act within this world on the basis of its own state (data, attributes, and/or methods)'.

In addition, there is no shortage of undergraduate courses on ABM and we have some important texts for computational analysis in various disciplines,[6] but there is no 'general purpose' manual, so to speak, and we think this is due to the lack of a general formal theory. At the same time there are different environments for the development of agent modelling (Section 2.1): while this is a source of inexhaustible richness for the development of ABM as a discipline, it can also generate some bewilderment.

For a better understanding of some of the reasons for this dissatisfaction it is also important to make a distinction between the concepts of 'simulation' and 'computation', often considered as synonyms. Greenblat (1971) claims that:

> A simulation is an 'operating model' of central features or elements of a real or
> proposed system, process, or environment. .... it is not the entire system that is

---

[6] Among a wider list of books, we recommend Billari et al. (2006), Tesfatsion and Judd (2006), Wilensky and Rand (2015), Hamill and Gilbert (2016), Cioffi-Revilla (2017), and Railsback and Grimm (2019).

modeled or represented, but only selected features. What is important is that the model 'behaves' like the referent system … for what is essential is that a simulation is a 'dynamic' model. As changes take place in the referent system, they likewise take place in the model; functional as well as structural relationships in the simulation are isomorphic with those of the referent system. (p. 161)

Both the simulation and the computation are based on the execution of a model by means of a suitably instructed calculator but, differently from the simulation, the computation does not need a model which is a formalised representation of a real fact. These computational experiments return results, but of little practical value; however, they are not entirely without value from an analytical and methodological perspective. For example, the Shelling model of social segregation or Conway's *Game of Life* are computational experiments, and it is on this basis that Epstein and Axtell's (1996) *Sugarscape* model was developed. Similarly, it is from 'toy models' of the economy that actual simulation experiments were then developed, such as the CATS model (Delli Gatti et al., 2011), the EURACE models (Cincotti et al., 2010; Dawid et al., 2018) and, more recently, the CAN-ABM (Next-Generation Agent-Based Model of Canada) model of Hommes et al. (2021) and the model of Poledna et al. (2020) for predicting the macroeconomic effects of the COVID-related lockdown in Austria.

Mainstream economics remains sceptical because it sees ABMS as black boxes with too many degrees of freedom that would allow anything to be supported. Our position, on the other hand, is that such models are fully transparent and microfounded by construction, the assumptions are explicit and so are the equations that implement them. From a theoretical point of view, there is all the potential needed to overcome the limitations of the *mainstream* method and orient research towards the Economics of Complexity, and from an applicative point of view we have formal bases, even if not yet consolidated and shared, that allow us to propose ABM as a reference methodology even though validation is in the making, as we shall see in Section 2.3.

1.4 Some History

The origins of agent modelling are often traced back to Orcutt's 1957 work on microsimulation (Ballot et al., 2015). This work aims to understand the economic consequences of welfare and redistributive policies. In Orcutt's model there are many heterogeneous agents interacting without centralised guidance, the simulation results can be computed numerically, and the system is dynamic and recursive. But the absence of a market is a major limitation to the completeness of the model. Two economists tried to remedy this simultaneously, with consistent stock flow models that place great emphasis on the initialisation and calibration process. Bergmann (1974) published the TRANSACTIONS model, capable of generating aggregate macroeconomic outcomes. Eliasson in 1977 and 1984, constructed MOSES, a model of the Swedish economy. This is a forerunner of many ABM models, inspired by Schumpeter – innovations and business demography; Keynes – relations between demand for goods and consumer-labour income; and Wicksell – adaptive expectations and limited rationality of agents. It lays the foundation on which later ABMS will build their elaborations.

Turrell (2013, p. 175) reminds us that the first model with agents, although not according to the current view, was developed by Enrico Fermi in the 1930s.

> The initial spur for developing agent-based models came in the 1930s when physicist Enrico Fermi was trying to solve problems involving the transport of neutrons, a sub-atomic particle, through matter. Neutron transport was difficult to model as each step in a neutron's journey is probabilistic: there is a chance the particle will directly interact with, scatter off, or pass-by other particles. Previous methods had tried to capture the aggregate behaviour of all the neutrons at once, but the immense number of different possibilities for neutron paths through matter made the problem very challenging.
>
> Fermi developed a new method to solve these problems in which he treated the neutrons individually, using a mechanical adding machine to perform the computations for each individual neutron in turn. The technique involved generating random numbers and comparing them to the probabilities derived from theory. If the probability of a neutron colliding were 0.8, and he generated a random number smaller than 0.8, he allowed a 'simulated' neutron to collide. Similar techniques were used to find the outgoing direction of the neutron after the collision. By doing this repeatedly, and for a large number of simulated neutrons, Fermi could build up a picture of the real way that neutrons would pass through matter. Fermi took great delight in astonishing his colleagues with the accuracy of his predictions without, initially, revealing his trick of treating the neutrons like agents.
>
> The agent-based techniques Fermi and colleagues developed went on to play an important role in the development of nuclear weapons and nuclear power. At around the same time that Fermi was developing his technique, the first electronic computers were becoming available at the world's leading scientific institutions. Computing power remains key to agent-based modelling today, with some of the world's supercomputers being harnessed for ever more detailed simulations.
>
> By 1947 scientists had developed a name for this technique which reflected its probabilistic nature: the Monte Carlo method. The story goes that the name was inspired by Stanislaw Ulam's uncle, who would often ask to borrow money by saying he 'just had to go to Monte Carlo'. In 1949, Metropolis and Ulam published a paper together entitled 'The Monte Carlo Method' which explained the many uses of the new technique of using random numbers to tackle problems. Not all of these were agent-based models but all relied on using artificially generated random numbers to solve problems. This more general Monte Carlo technique has been applied very widely, for instance to calculating solutions to equations with many parameters, to the management of risk and catastrophes, and to investments in finance.

The more general Monte Carlo method has the strength that it can very efficiently explore a large number of possibilities. For instance, the usual way for Fermi's neutron problem to have been treated would have been to create a grid of every single possibility and then fill in what happens for each of them. This means that even implausibly unlikely scenarios are computed. Monte Carlo instead focuses on the most likely outcomes. This property can make the difference to whether a particular problem is solvable or not. The Monte Carlo method can also deal with distributions, for instance across income, which are not described by a normal distribution.

The simulation to which Fermi refers is closer to the so-called Monte Carlo method than to the ABM methodology.

Von Neumann proposed a theoretical machine capable of reproducing itself, which is often remembered as the first example of a computational agent model. The Polish mathematician suggested that the machine was described by a set of cells on a grid, and based on this intuition (von Neumann, 1951) created what later literature would call 'cellular automata'. Another step forward is Conway's *Game of Life* (Gardner, 1970), which operates with simple rules of interaction between agents that are identical except for their geographical location on a two-dimensional chessboard. Conway can show that, depending on various initial conditions, 'regular' aggregate structures emerge. One of the first models based on interacting heterogeneous agents was Thomas Schelling's (1971) segregation model that produces an aggregate emergent result starting from individual disorder. In Figure 1 a simulation result of Schelling's model is represented. Agents are initially placed on a physical grid at random: 10 per cent of the cells are maintained empty while the remaining 90 per cent of the cells are occupied by blue and red agents in equal shares. The main behaviour is that each individual likes living close to a given share of agents of the same colour, say 25 per cent. At any iteration agents seek similar agents, and all of them move until this fraction is satisfied for everyone: there is no guarantee that the simulation ends. If the simulation ends, take this as an initial condition, increase the similarity required, say up to 50 per cent, and run the model again. If this second simulation ends, that is, the share is reached for every agent, some segregation is observable. Assume this as an initial condition, increase the similarity up to 75 per cent, and run the model again: if it ends, the artificial society appears more segregated.

A decade later, Robert Axelrod (1997) presented a model in the form of a tournament of strategies of the prisoner's dilemma to determine a winner. It was Craig Reynolds (1987) who developed some of the first models based on biological agents – later known as artificial life – that contain social features, while a pioneering ABM paper was by Kim and Markowitz (1989) and the follow-up research by Jacobs et al. (2004).

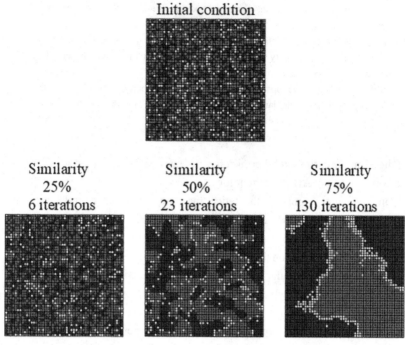

Figure 1 A simulation result of Schelling's model.
Parameters: Red/Blue 45%/45%; Empty 10%; Size 50×50; Delay 100 ms.
Simulations retrieved from http://nifty.stanford.edu/2014/mccown-schelling-model-segregation/.

For a short history of Agent-Based Computational Economics (ACE) see Tasfatsion (2021). As a variant of ABM, the c-ABM (Box 1) finds ACE as its own special case because it is a method of modelling the real world according to the principles of c-ABM. An ACE model is an 'initial-value state-space modeling of an economic system' (Tesfatsion, 2021) because it fulfils the principles of c-ABM and does not involve schemes of rationality, optimality and equilibrium that depend on the ideas of the researcher, but consists only of 'logically contructive autonomous agents interacting within a modeled system satisfying system constructivity and system historicity'.

The last decade of the last century saw the expansion of ABM within the social sciences with the 'Sugarscape model' of Joshua M. Epstein and Robert Axtell (1996) and especially the spread of the Santa Fe Institute approach that became popular from the 1980s onwards under the influence of research on complex adaptive systems (CAS) modelling. This research adopts a transdisciplinary focus on the general phenomenology of complex adaptive systems in biology, economics, technology, and society. If up to this point the history of ABMS is primarily a US story, in 1999 Nigel Gilbert and Klaus Troitzsch published their book *Simulation for the Social Scientist* (Gilbert and Troitzsch, 1999) and founded the *Journal of Artificial Societies and Social Simulation* (JASSS). Shortly before this, the international *Workshop on Economics with Heterogeneous Interacting Agents* (WEHIA) was organised in Ancona in 1996 (Gallegati and Kirman, 2019).

Beyond this, the reading proposed by Squazzoni (2010; p. 200) seems convincing to us. According to Squazzoni while the interdisciplinary Santa Fe Institute (SFI) approach dominates in the US:

> in Europe, it has been metabolized prima facie by some innovative social scientists working within and to some extent between their own disciplines, who saw it as 'the' social science modelling technique par excellence that, once applied to traditional scientific questions, would strengthen the explanatory power of the social sciences and improve them from within.

Currently, ABM methodology is increasingly successful also in economics: a scientific society (ESHIA, Economic Sciences with Heterogeneous Interacting Agents), a dedicated journal (JEIC, *Journal of Economic Interaction and Co-ordination*), books (Delli Gatti et al., 2018; *Handbook of Computational Economics*, in four vols., 1996, 2006, 2014, 2018, Elsevier; while Cambridge University Press publishes a series of Elements devoted to Complexity and ABM, one of which you are reading), an internationally relevant PhD school at Sant'Anna in Pisa, conferences (WEHIA), research centres (Cattolica in Milan, Oxford, Vienna and many others) and papers in top 50 journals, which have quadrupled in the last 10 years. Moreover, Andrew Sheng reminds us, in an interview with Project Sindacate on 24 March 2020, that

> the agent-based models China is using now are multidisciplinary, multilevel models – what nuclear physicist Qian Xuesen has called 'giant open complex system' models. They remain crude, but with sufficient data and appropriate artificial intelligence tools – which China is collecting and developing, respectively – one can look for 'knowable unknowns' and provide better options.

In Italy, at least four universities have developed ABM themes: Genoa with EURACE, a large Stock-Flow Consistent (SFC) model with European data (Cincotti et al., 2010, 2012); the Cattolica University in Milan with CATS that integrates finance with production (Delli Gatti et al., 2005, 2011) and now proposes 'hybrid' models (Assenza et al., 2013, 2015); the Sant'Anna in Pisa with the K+S (Keynes+Schumpeter) model (Dosi et al., 2010, 2013), where the introduction and diffusion of innovations and their effects on the structure of the economy are masterfully modelled and heterogeneous capital goods adequately considered, and has produced many other works where great attention is devoted to networks, policy and empirical verification;[7] and finally Ancona, where a number of researchers have contributed to produce the CATS, the 'ABModellaccio' (Caiani et al., 2016; Caiani and Caverzasi, 2017) and the 'Modellone' (Riccetti et al., 2015; Russo et al., 2016).

2 Tools for the Simulation with Models Based on Agents

For the simulation of agent-based models (ABMS) there are two possibilities. The first one is that one writes a program with some programming language so as to construct all the necessary components, that is, the implementation of the agents specifying the property (data and behaviors); the interface with which the observer (researcher) interacts with the model in order to set the parameters, to import data (if necessary) and to export the results; and the interface with which to proceed to the statistical analysis of the results and to visualise them. This solution is the 'freest' one because it allows a high degree of customisation, especially if a 'general purpose language' is chosen, and it allows one to treat agents with a high degree of autonomy, very close to the notion of real agent as far as the structure of their state and behaviours are concerned. However, this is also the most difficult way, especially if you do not have computer science and programming skills, typically according to the OOP (Object-Oriented Programming) paradigm. Usually, you just write a program to implement the agents and let them act, after setting some parameters, while the study of the results is conducted with other tools after exporting them in some format. A similar, but in fact different, solution is to use Computational Mathematics Systems, such as *Mathematica* or MATLAB,[8] which are integrated development environments for numerical computation and graphical representation (Macal, 2004).

The other, more common, option is to adopt a dedicated ABMS platform. In general, the ideal simulation system should provide the following features:

- minimal learning effort to use,
- maximum flexibility to build simulation models,
- as much standardisation as possible,
- stable but continuously developing libraries and packages,

---

[7] The K+S model can replicate the stylised facts of system behaviour at multiple levels (micro, meso and macro; Delli Gatti et al., 2007). Since ABM models are multi-level, consistency between empirical evidence and theoretical prescriptions is crucial. The 'principle of unreality' that Simon (1963) attributes to Friedman (1953), namely, that a model might be useful at the aggregate level while being wrong at the level of the agents, does not apply.

[8] *Mathematica* is a registered trademark of Wolfram Research Inc., www.wolfram.com. Some examples of ABMS with Mathematica are available in the site https://demonstrations.wolfram .com/topic.html?limit=20&topic=Multi-agent+Modeling. See also https://library.wolfram.com/ infocenter/Conferences/5767/#downloads. MATLAB is a registered trademark of The MathWorks Inc., www.mathworks.com.

- the most agile user interaction,
- analysis tools, including visual ones, and
- maximum portability on different machines and operating systems (Abar et al., 2017).

Currently, no single platform meets all these requirements at the highest level. If several programming languages are available, some at no or low cost, then far more platforms are available for the ABMS. The solution of adopting a platform greatly simplifies the work but imposes a difficult choice even before starting it. In fact, there is no best platform, but it is possible to find the most suitable one according to our goals. The choice depends on various factors. Some factors are, so to speak, exogenous to the project. For example, if it seems that platform X is better than platform Y for some reason, we must also consider whether and which of the two is distributed under a commercial license, which implies costs, rather than open-source, whether it is freeware or shareware, and for what purposes the software we are going to produce is allowed and its possibility of distribution. This first aspect is important but not the most difficult to address. In fact, since there is no best platform, we must immediately keep in mind what is the purpose for which we implement the model and its structure. That is, the scale, understood as the number of agents we want to implement, the variety of agent species that populate the ecology of the model, the degree of complexity of the agents, and the modelling of the environment itself. Moreover, we must also consider that some platforms are maintained, with continuous evolutions and developments, as the computer science and the calculators evolve, while others are never updated and, therefore, they can become obsolete or unusable on recent computers.

The typical elements one needs in ABMS are:

- a tool for implementing agents and building the environment in which they operate,
- an event generation tool,
- a tool for setting parameters – or importing data if needed – and
- a tool for analysing and visualising results.

With few exceptions, almost all available platforms meet these requirements. All platforms are based on a programming language, which facilitates code control, reuse, and distribution. Almost all ABMS platforms owe a debt to the progenitor, the Swarm platform built by Langton for the simulation of artificial life as a complement to traditional biology (Langton, 1995).

An ABMS platform is therefore a computational environment, based on a programming language, with which it is possible to encode a model written 'pen and paper' in a computer-executable program to study some phenomenon or the dynamics of a system, without having to deal too much with the computer aspects, that is having few or no programming skills.

2.1 Some of the Mostly Diffused ABMS Platforms

With the growing interest in ABMS in all areas of research, there has been a proliferation of programming languages and dedicated platforms. Some are more suitable for building prototype models, simple, even educational, low-cost and distributable without too many constraints, frequently referred to as 'toy models'. These platforms aim at the immediate use of the model with low software learning costs, but this advantage is paid in terms of model scalability and low execution efficiency. Others are instead more appropriate for developing applied research models, sometimes quite complex, that require great computing power and speed, sometimes imply costs, and pose restrictions for distribution, especially for commercial purposes. Choosing which platform to adopt also is relevant, because some limitations in model development and future revisions or extensions may depend on this choice. Currently, we have many review articles in the literature regarding operational tools for the ABMS and this section does not aspire to be added to the list. The purpose here is instead to provide a bibliographic base for further study and briefly present some of the most used platforms such as Swarm, Repast, Mason, NetLogo and EcoLab; for the many others that we do not mention here, we refer to the literature that we will discuss.

There is common agreement in the ABMS user community that Swarm (Minar et al., 1996) is the progenitor of all dedicated platforms.[9] Swarm was conceived in the mid-1990s by Christopher Langton to implement a model without having to deal with computer science, namely, without having to set up calculation tools, parameters management, agent initialisation, analysis, and visualisation. Everything had to be integrated in a single environment so that one could focus only on the model. The first versions were based on procedural programming languages such as C and FORTRAN, but those were also the times when the OOP paradigm was starting to spread, so the development of Swarm proceeded in Objective-C and C++.[10] At present Swarm includes three components: ModelSwarm is the computational implementation tool for the model, ObserverSwarm is the tool with which the researcher can analyse and visualise the results, and BatchSwarm is the tool to store and investigate results, data, and parameters. There is also a Java-Swarm version, but it is less wide-spread than other platforms that are based on the Java language natively.[11] In

---

[9] www.swarm.org.

[10] https://en.wikipedia.org/wiki/Objective-C; https://en.wikipedia.org/wiki/C%2B%2B.

[11] https://en.wikipedia.org/wiki/Java_(programming_language).

various ways, all platforms inherit from Swarm part of the basic philosophy and several tools, even if they are developed with different languages. For example, after Swarm many implement a 'discrete event scheduler', which allows agents to trigger their behaviours at given times, and the ability to implement a physical space, mapping it to a 2D grid, on which to place agents. A recent development of this platform is SLAPP (Swarm-Like Agent Protocol in Python) which is based on Python, and conceived and maintained by Pietro Terna (2019).[12]

The REPAST (Recursive Porous Agent Simulation Toolkit) platform was introduced by Sallach, Collier, Howe, and Nelson (North et al., 2006).[13] REPAST is a platform that owes a lot to Swarm, and it is proposed in three variants: RepastJ is based on Java, Repast.Net is based on C#[14] in the Microsoft .Net environment, and RepastPy is the latest development in Python. Like Swarm, REPAST also has a discrete event scheduler, a graphical interface (GUI) to manage variables and parameters, an analysis and visualisation tool, and a tool for spatial localisation of the agents in a simple way (2D grid) or a realistic way (networks and GIS).[15] It also has a tool to use genetic algorithms and neural networks useful for parameter calibration. Although younger than Swarm, REPAST is also extensively documented, making it particularly attractive.

The MASON (Multi-Agent Simulator of Neighborhoods) platform was introduced in 2003 (Luke et al., 2005) as an ABMS platform fully developed in Java.[16] More so than Swarm and REPAST, MASON is capable of handling large-scale models and has 3D visualisation tools. Being younger, it is less widely used, its documentation is reduced, and it also requires more learning effort to use, making it less attractive than previous platforms, but the number of its users is growing.

NetLogo is a platform conceived by Wilensky (1999) for ABMS; it is widely diffused because mainly aimed for didactical purposes, and so it is very easy to use.[17] As its heir StarLogo is based on the Logo logic developed in the second half of the 1960s.[18] Its simplicity and its main educational goal do not make it an ideal tool for realistic and large-scale simulation; however, it does not require any computer or programming skills and, in any case, many research models

---

[12] https://en.wikipedia.org/wiki/Python_(programming language); https://terna.github.io/SLAPP/.

[13] https://repast.github.io/index.html.

[14] https://en.wikipedia.org/wiki/C_Sharp_;(programming_language).

[15] https://en.wikipedia.org/wiki/Geographic_information_system.

[16] https://cs.gmu.edu/~eclab/projects/mason/.

[17] https://ccl.northwestern.edu/netlogo/; http://ccl.northwestern.edu/netlogo-ccl.shtml.

[18] https://education.mit.edu/project/starlogo-tng/; http://web.mit.edu/mitstep/starlogo/index.html; https://en.wikipedia.org/wiki/Logo_(programming_language).

have been developed in this environment. Currently also available is the OpenStarLogo version, an open-source release based on Java.

EcoLab is an advanced ABMS platform introduced by Standish and Leow (2003) and owes its name to a research project dedicated to the dynamics of evolution.[19] The EcoLab platform is developed in C++ and requires C++ programming skills to implement the models. Although it is sufficiently documented, the references are mostly based on specific research models. All this makes EcoLab less attractive than other solutions for different research fields, especially in the social sciences. One of EcoLab's strengths is that it can handle large-scale models, that is, with millions of agents, because its applications can be distributed over a network of computers by exploiting the power of parallel computing.

2.2 A Guide to the Literature on ABMS Tools

The main goal of this section is to provide a guide to the literature on tools for ABMS so that the researcher can find himself facilitated in choosing the most suitable platform for the project. The logic we will adopt is 'historical,' that is, we will start with the most recent review and work our way back to the oldest. As will be noticed, the necessity to pass in review the various tools is parallel to the increasing interest for the ABMS, in all the fields of search, that has determined its proliferation. Many other reviews are available, but the ones we will discuss here are those we consider most general. It will also be noted that we can define a set of platforms that all the reviews discussed deal with, but each provides details that are only hinted at by others. In the bibliographical references of each contribution, one will be able to find the reviews that we do not discuss here.

To our knowledge, the most recent and comprehensive review on platforms for ABM development is that of Pal et al. (2020), which describes the main characteristics of two families of platforms. As far as the 'general purpose' platforms are concerned, 36 are described, of which 26 are open-source and 10 commercial. For the 'special purpose' platforms, 48 are described, almost all open-source. Finally, there are also 50 platforms whose status and license are unclear. At present we can therefore conclude that more than 132 platforms are available and the authors for each one report the reference language, the website, the type of license and a brief description of the use. In addition to this remarkable review effort, the authors also offer a brief history of agent-based systems and the main fields of application.

---

[19] http://ecolab.sourceforge.net/ecolab.html.

Abar et al. (2017) describe 86 platforms, specifying, for each, the reference language, the types of agents and interactive behavior, the language or Application Programming Interface (API) for development and the possibility of an Integrated Development Environment (IDE), the compiler, the operating system that supports it and the type of computer on which it can be run, the modelling capability and scalability of the models, and finally, providing a brief description of the field of use. In this study, there is also a very important section (section 4.1) devoted to the general criteria for comparing the platforms.

Leon et al. (2015) propose a review of the tools for ABMS by grouping them into five broad categories: (1) 23 General Purpose Platforms, (2) 6 Modelling and Simulation Platforms, (3) 8 Special Purpose Platforms, (4) 40 Platforms No Longer Under Development, and finally (5) a list of 14 Methodologies for Multiagent Systems Development. In each of the categories 1 through 4 they identify projects in existence from those that have been suspended or whose status is unclear. Compared to the reviews, for each of these categories it provides less technical detail but proposes a broader description, including additional references and information.

The review of Kravari and Bassiliades (2015) is different from those just presented. In fact, although proposing a list of 24 platforms, this contribution puts a lot of attention on a list of 'universal criteria' with which to classify them. The authors explain that they installed all the platforms they analysed and for each one they performed some experiments based on the available 'tutorials', to evaluate the slope of the learning curve for each tool. Without going into details we briefly report the five evaluation criteria adopted: (1) Platform Properties: 'basic characteristics that are necessary for a potential user/developer in order to understand the scope and the domain of the platform'; (2) Usability: 'suitability of the platform for the construction of agent applications'; (3) Operating Ability (quality): 'aspects that are taken into account during execution'; (4) Pragmatics: 'external factors that are neither related to the construction nor to the operation of the platform'; (5) Security Management: 'security issues, indicating if the platform is considered safe or not'. The 24 platforms analysed are described in five synoptic tables, one for each of the preceding criteria. Finally, three additional criteria are considered: the programming language required for use, the FIPA (Foundation for Intelligent Physical Agents) Compliance,[20] although FIPA is now integrated into the IEEE (Institute of Electrical and Electronics Engineers) Computer Society,[21] the scope and possibility of using Semantic Web Technologies.

---

[20] www.fipa.org/.   [21] www.ieee.org/; www.computer.org/.

Bădică et al. (2011) propose a further alternative review because they also focus on the languages used to build the platforms and not only on the platforms. The authors provide a detailed description of 19 programming languages with which it is possible to implement Agent-Oriented Programming (AOP) tools that focus on the notion of 'agent' endowed with some characteristics such as 'mental qualities', 'communicative skills' and the 'notion of time'. In this regard, table 1 describes 37 'agent's features', of which in Sections 1.1 and 1.2 we have briefly discussed only a part. Agent-Oriented Programming is a specialisation of the OOP paradigm, and the authors highlight both the differences between 'agents' and 'objects' and how the AOP language

> provides a high level of abstraction directed towards developing agents and incorporates constructs for representing all the features defined by the frame-work. Most of all, it should allow developers to define agents and bind them to specific behaviors [87]; represent an agent's knowledge base, containing its mental state; and allow agents to communicate with each other.

The languages covered are grouped into three major categories: eight Agent-Oriented Programming Model, seven BDI based programming languages, and four Other Agent Languages. Very important is table 3, placed at the bottom of the text, which proposes a 'Summary of Agent Languages' for synoptic comparison according to seven criteria: the availability of a web site, the availability of an IDE, the implementation language, the agent platform integration, the field of application, the type of paradigm and, very important, the availability of a textbook of which, in bibliography, they report the references. After this description they also consider 13 platforms among the most popular at that time, which can still be valid today.

Allan (2010) describes 31 software packages and 13 multi-agent systems, in addition to collecting some applications in different fields. It also discusses the ABMS in the HPC (High Performance Computing) area.

Bordini et al. (2006) discuss three arguments: the languages, the Integrated Development Environments (IDEs), and the platforms. Languages are classified in three categories: (1) declarative, 'characterised by their strong formal nature, normally grounded on logic', (2) imperative, 'in practice agent notions are often implemented in an *ad hoc* manner', (3) hybrid, 'programming languages which are declarative while at the same time providing some specific constructs allow-ing for the use of code implemented in some external imperative language'. After that, eight IDEs are described. Integrated Development Environments focus on the programming language level and intend to enhance the productivity by automating tedious coding tasks. The authors propose five criteria for classifying IDEs based on functionality: project management, creating and editing source files, refactoring, build and run processes, and testing. Finally, they propose the description of five dedicated platforms.

A separate discourse deserves the review of Krešimir et al. (2020) because, to our knowledge, it is the only one dedicated to teaching tools, which makes it particularly interesting for the development of ABMS as a discipline. Because of this peculiarity, this review is different from all the others discussed here because it must also consider organisational aspects of teaching. In this contribution 17 didactic tools are described, among which there are those of the so-called Logo family, and a synoptic comparison is proposed based on six criteria: the type of license, the language or API, the possibility of IDE, the operating system, the type of computers on which it is possible to install them and the degree of complexity on a learning curve.

2.3 General Characteristics of an ABM

In dealing with ABM we resort to computer simulation, that is, programmable apparatuses that we can interrogate by means of an interface, to which we can provide inputs to obtain a response in a finite time. The formal development of economic theories can also make use of any real-valued functions, of non-finite sets or of countable infinities, but for their models to be made operational, namely, to be implemented in computer-executable programs on real data, it is necessary to base them constructively.[22]

In what follows we describe some of the main general characteristics that can be implemented in an ABM (Bonabeau, 2002) from the most particular elements, at the level of the agents – autonomy, heterogeneity, and interaction – to the more global ones, at the system level – discontinuity, discreteness, and flexibility.

Considering autonomous agents means that their actions are not coordinated by an auctioneer or a top-down centralised mechanism. In ABM, heterogeneity is both *between* agents – different species are considered, for example, firms and households – and *within* – all agents of the same species are not identical. Differences may concern *structural* aspects of the agents, related to their endowments or to states that may change during the simulation. Another aspect of heterogeneity that can be considered is related to *behavioural* aspects, such as preferences and methods of expectation formation (Hommes, 2013; Dosi, 2023;

---

[22] Constructivism is a way of doing mathematics which is based on Brower's intuitionist philosophy, according to which in mathematics there exist only objects of which it is possible to specify a mental construction. Thus, one cannot accept the existence of a mathematical object on a logical basis alone, but one must define a procedure for constructing it, hence demonstration by reductio ad absurdum cannot be accepted. This approach therefore leads to the rejection of a large part of classical mathematics, but lays the foundations for recursivity and computability, as an application of logic to computer science.

Palestrini et al., 2021) or learning methods (Sargent, 1993), see also Landini et al. (2014, 2015). With ABMS it is also possible to simulate anticipatory behaviour (Rosen, 1985), namely, of agents who, based on an expected scenario, prepare today the conditions to act tomorrow to obtain the expected result the day after tomorrow; see Di Guilmi et al. (2017) and the literature on evolutionary strategic games.

As explained in Section 1.2, an essential aspect of human behaviour that can be explicitly considered in ABMS is *direct interaction* (between agents). By *direct interaction* we mean the case of (at least) two counterparts meeting to interact. Not infrequently, the simulation of these relational processes follows probabilistic rules to generalise these processes in a plausible way. For example, given the units of the system one can assume that each one is randomly coupled with a subset of counterparts to interact with. The interaction can be represented in a network where the agents are the nodes, and the interactions are the links. In the case of indirect interaction there are no links between agents, but only links between them and the 'market'. With interaction comes an essential component of complexity, connectivity (Casti, 1979; Wassermann and Faust, 2008; Scott and Carrington, 2011; Caldarelli and Catanzaro, 2012; Knoke and Yang, 2019). Note that direct interaction is one of the holistic factors that inhibit reductionism (see Box 2 in Landini et al., 2024), the other being feedbacks.

The agents of an ABM simulating a socio-economic system are autonomous, heterogeneous, and interacting in a diversified multi-level network structure. Under these conditions it is possible that some individuals change their preference patterns, opinions or orient their decisions differently to such an extent that a discontinuity is created. In an ABM it is possible to simulate the introduction of innovations that create discontinuities, far beyond the idea of an exogenous *shock*. These and other examples of discontinuities are explicitly simulated in an AB-Model (Bellomo et al., 2020; Giordano et al., 2020; Pescarmona et al., 2020). If we simulate individuals with differential equations the discontinuity would be difficult to observe, except in the case of some chaotic models, and the alternative would be to use stochastic jump processes, whose trajectories are continuous at least to the right. Instead, with agent simulation, precisely because it implements a structure of logic gates in the emulation of decision processes, it is possible to explicitly take account of actual discontinuities right from the micro level.

An ABM must be completely characterised by the discreteness of its dimensions: the events it describes are discrete because they occur at distinct times on a discrete and finite time horizon and in discrete and finite space, if only because these are the limits imposed by the limited numerical calculation capacity of computers. Thus, each agent is a discrete-event decision machine, which in its actions simulates real processes as a sequence of discrete events in time and space, be it a mapping of physical space or a topological space.

In an ABM the equations of motion that describe the evolution of the agents' characteristics over time are finite horizon difference equations, linking the outcomes of events occurring at time $t - 1$ with those of time t, on which those of time $t + 1$ will depend. Sometimes different phenomena follow different *clocks*, for example, the worker serves every day, is paid at the end of the month, but spends on consumption every day. With reference to space, we have more topics because different types of space can be considered explicitly in an ABM. The mapping of a physical space may consist in locating the units of the system on a real geographical space but on a reduced scale. One can also consider a fictitious geography: grid structures (*lattice*) – typically two-dimensional – in which to locate agents. A more abstract perspective employs networks (or graphs) in which nodes represent given locations, for example, interchange points for commuting, communication, or exchange of goods and information. Finally, a further perspective defines a topological space of states whose degrees of freedom are established by the state quantities that characterise the states of individual agents. For example, let us assume that we can distinguish between large and small firms: $X_1 = \{x_{1,1} = \text{big}; x_{1,2} = \text{small}\}$. In addition, firms may be indebted or financially self-sufficient: $X_2 = \{x_{2,1} = \text{indebted}; x_{2,2} = \text{aut-archic}\}$. We can now construct a two-dimensional state space $S_2 = X_1 \times X_2$ that results in a table of four cells; individual firm-agents can migrate from one status cell to another. Each cell is then identifiable with a state vector $\mathbf{w}_h = (x_{i,1}, x_{j,2})$, and each can host a given number N_h of agents. Thus, by coupling the state vector to its occupation number $\mathbf{m}_h = (\mathbf{w}_h, N_h)$ we can describe the micro-state of the system $\mathbf{M} = \{\mathbf{m}_h : h = 1, \ldots, H\}$. Therefore, due to subsequent decisions – actions of autonomous agents that are heterogeneous and interacting – along the simulation, we can describe the system's evolution through time $\mathbf{m}_{h,t} = (\mathbf{w}_{h,t}, N_{h,t})$. This method is generalisable to many dimensions and builds a bridge of communication between ABM as a *simulation laboratory for complex systems* and the methods of statistical physics appropriate to the description of complex systems (Di Guilmi et al., 2017).

Agent-Based Modelling is very flexible in several respects. First, the basic model can be enriched with a larger number of agents, thus enlarging the scale. This can be useful, for example, to assess whether the model is robust with respect to scale and whether it develops coordination phenomena or *self-organised criticality* (see Box 5 in Landini et al., 2024). We can also enrich the model from a behavioural point of view by specifying more decision rules. Furthermore, it is possible to extend the number of agent species by taking the model to a higher level of *complexity*. Thus, from a basic model we can extend its *scale*, make the behaviour of agents more sophisticated and make the system more and more complex by extending its 'ecology' to capture and describe emerging phenomena and find more and more correspondence to the stylised facts. There is also another aspect of flexibility that is worth considering, *portability*: any ABM can be specified with paper and pencil and can then be implemented on the computer at low cost, both with many dedicated agent simulation environments and with a wide range of programming languages, both low- and high-level, thus being able to operate, overcoming the rigidities of dedicated environments.

2.4 Validation

The social sciences study situated phenomena that happen under given conditions in space and time. Many of these phenomena are not replicable, either because the conditions change over time or because they are not found identically in space, or because they emerge from below in an unpredictable way. Also, for these reasons, the explanation of facts in the social sciences occurs through interpretive models, not necessarily quantitative, that represent facts based on one or more theories. In economics, but not only, a theoretical-conceptual model can have practical, empirical use, especially when it is translated into a program executable by a computer. In all cases, a model is always a partial representation of a situated phenomenon and considers only the elements thought to be essential to explain the facts, neglecting many details that can be treated in future developments. In such a sense, every model is formulated for understanding a simplified representation of the reality, useful for understanding the principles at the bottom of it, and this also applies to this theory.[23]

For a real fact several models can be specified, even based on the same reference theory. In the social sciences, there is no 'right' theory to interpret facts nor is there an 'exact' model to describe them. Moreover, different methodologies can be adopted to specify different models even from the point of view of the same theory. Not infrequently, one has several theories of reference, sometimes complementary but also alternative. A problem then arises. If for the same fact you can have different theories from which descend models methodologically different, then the question is how to assess the goodness of the theoretical implications and results of a model to establish the best possible explanation, at least until proven otherwise.

---

[23] Parisi (2006) invites us to reflect on the fact that even Descartes assumed the absence of friction to describe the motion of bodies, although in a world without friction we could not be alive: we could not move or feed ourselves; in fact, food would escape from our hands, assuming we were able to get a hold on it.

If among the various models available we can isolate the one we consider the 'best', then we also know its methodology and we can even go back to its theory that, therefore, we can consider as the most appropriate. The issue is very complex because to evaluate the goodness of the results of different models that transcribe different theories sometimes different evaluation protocols are needed.

We now narrow our focus to the class of agent-based models. In this area, the evaluation practice is called *validation* because its purpose is *to assess whether the model can be considered a valid factual knowledge base*. It is not impossible that two different agent-based models, implementing two alternative theories, can be valid knowledge bases. However, if a model is validated in the sense previously mentioned, and that we will elaborate in what follows, then it can be considered a scientific tool. Consequently, with a validated model we can do experiments and sometimes even extrapolate predictions to further the knowledge we have. If a model is validated, then it provides empirical support for the theory it implements and allows for further development. In any case, it is good to be aware, a theory supported by a validated model will be a valid basis of knowledge until proven otherwise, both in the natural and social sciences.

In the social sciences, but not only, the model does not have to be exhaustive of reality, nor is it relevant that it is very sophisticated. What matters is the rigor with which it has been specified and with which it is able to answer research questions and explain a part of the mechanisms that the theory supposes are at the base of the phenomena it deals with. Even a simple model with few goals can provide a valid knowledge base if it passes validation. The specification of a model can be considered as a moment along the path of (social) research with scientific method and rigor. Furthermore, a (social) simulation model that is validated can be a computational laboratory, and computer simulation can play the same role that empirical experimentation plays for natural, life, or engineering sciences.

Validation is the crucial step that closes the development of an ABM model. As important as it is, there is no standard validation protocol, no procedure unanimously agreed upon by the scientific community, nor are all ABMS validated. What we do have is an evolving but poorly standardised set of 'best practices' or 'guidelines'. In fact, validation is an area of research in continuous development.[24] There is no lack of procedures, nor of innovative ideas. What is

---

[24] Beyond the books of Gilbert (2020) and Rand and Rust (2011), we consider particularly important the contributions of Borgonovo et al. (2022), Platt (2020), Fagiolo and Richiardi (2018), Richiardi (2018), Colasante (2017), Bargigli (2017), Stonedahl and Rand (2012), Borrill and Tesfatsion (2010), Frank et al. (2009), Bianchi et al. (2008), Windrum et al. (2007), and Leombruni et al. (2006).

Table 1 A summary diagram of the validation process

	Consistency	**Correctness**

Evaluation	1 VERIFICATION:
	A. Programmatic
	   testing
	   A.1 Unit testing
	   A.2 Code
	   walkthroughs
		3 FALSIFICATION:
		  C. Test cases:
		    C.1 Corner cases
		    C.2 Sampled cases
		    C.3 Specific scenarios
		  D. Micro-face *validation*
		  E. Meso-face *validation*
		  F. Macro-face *validation*
		  G. Empirical output
		    validation
		    G.1 Stylised facts
		    G.2 Real-world data
		    G.3 Cross-validation

Conformation	2 CONTROL:
	B. Programmatic testing
	   B.1 Debugging
	   walkthroughs
	   B.2 Formal Testing
		4 PARAMETRIZATION:
		  H. Test cases:
		    H.1 Relative value
		    testing
		  I. Empirical input *validation*

needed is a systematisation of the literature on validation, also starting from a shared definition of at least the main concepts and terms. Our aim is to present an interpretative scheme, and logically ordered, of the various steps with which to proceed to the validation process.

Validating an ABM means adopting a set of replicable procedures to 'conform' the results and 'evaluate' their conformity to given evaluative criteria. Mainly, the evaluation criteria we isolate are 'correctness', as the correspondence between the results and the actual data or shared knowledge, and 'consistency', as correspondence between the specification of the model and the theory, checking for possible contradictions. By combining procedures and criteria we attempt to logically organise a 'validation process' largely drawing from Gilbert (2020) and Rand and Rust (2011) according to the following scheme (Table 1).

We introduce a general definition: *the validation of a model is the process of evaluating the goodness of the results of a model to determine whether it can be considered a valid knowledge base.* Understood as a 'process', validation is a succession of logically ordered steps. One can also consider that the validation of a model proceeds in parallel to its formalisation and the development of the code. In fact, there are some tricks that can be followed from the beginning, such as taking extreme care both in formalising and writing the code, avoiding ambiguities to make everything as readable as possible even for those who do not participate in the project. In the writing of the code, it is important to accompany it with many comments that explain the various passages, that can be very useful in the transfer of the code between the various groups of development of the project, or in order to render it public, that is, ready to be used by other researchers, or in order to remember quickly what is being executed in given passages in the forecast to resume the model in the future. Different 'assertions', that is, messages that alert the programmer during the execution, as an example when some returned values are not admissible, can be inserted. Besides, to quickly identify conceptual errors of programming it can be useful to make intermediate outputs return to the program, especially for those sections that will not have to return results.

1. The 'verification' of a model is the 'evaluation with respect to consistency' to ensure that the model does what the theory prescribes. A model is verified when it formally and operationally decodes a theory, also from the point of view of calculation programs. Verification must precede all other steps. If a model does not represent the theory, then it must be reformulated. In the same way, if the program does not implement the logic of the model, then it must be cured. After verification, the theory, the model and the program may be considered as synonymous.

   There are some steps that can be considered in the verification. Having established that the conceptual model and the formalised model match, two tests can be conducted. The 'programmatic tests' of verification concern the code of the program that implements the model. Between these, the 'unit testing' consists in predisposing a specific test for every section of the code, as it is being written to verify that there are not procedural errors. Once a section has been verified, we proceed with the development and testing of the next one so that each section performs as expected. The 'code walkthroughs' consist in gathering a group of scholars of the theme in object to discuss with the programmer the entire code and to verify the logical correspondence between the conceptual model and the program.

2. The 'control' of a model is the 'conformation with respect to consistency', namely, the search for and removal of all possible contradictions. We say then that a model is controlled when it is free of logical contradictions. Control 'programmatic tests' are used to check that the implemented model performs what the programmer thinks it should. Among these, 'debugging walkthroughs' consist of running the program with the purpose of checking that it generates results correctly. 'Formal tests' employ logic tools to check that there are no

contradictions in the implemented formal model; sometimes agent models are very large and so complex that formal tests are difficult to perform.

3. The 'falsification' of a model is the 'evaluation with respect to empirical correctness', namely the construction of the model as the experimental moment of a theory. We say that a model, and thus its theory, is falsifiable if we can use it to perform an experiment whose results are comparable with the available data. Thus, by means of its verified model, the theory becomes falsifiable and assumes scientific connotation (see Box 12 in Landini et al., 2024).

In this area of validation there are several tests that can be conducted. Test cases are of various types. Among these, the 'corner cases' use extreme values of some inputs to evaluate if the program returns sensible results even in 'stressed' situations, for example considering a minimum number of agents or the maximum number allowed in the execution of the model. The 'sampled cases tests' are preparations of some inputs of which we do not know the outcomes until we execute the program but of which we have an idea about the range of variation of the values that will be returned in output. In this case the evaluation is positive if the results on some quantities of interest do not exceed the limits that we expect. If for input data it is known from the conceptual model what the outputs must be, then we conduct the 'specific scenarios test to estimate if the implemented model is able to reproduce them. This type of test is one of the first ones you run, but it is rather weak and is not in itself sufficient to guarantee that the code is bug-free' (Gilbert, 2020; p. 61).

At this stage of the evaluation process, three sorts of validation can be considered. The 'micro-face validation' consists in evaluating if the agents of the model, their behaviours and their properties correspond in a satisfactory way to the agents of the real world. The 'macro-face validation' consists in evaluating if the aggregate dynamics returned by the model correspond to real aggregate dynamics.

> In both micro- and macro-face validation, no data are directly compared to the model: instead, the focus is on showing that the general patterns, attributes, and processes have an explainable correspondence to the real world. It is usually sufficient to describe the relationship between the model and the world to show that it has been validated 'on face'. (Rand and Rust, 2011; p. 189)

Finally, the 'empirical output validation' is the phase considered most important because it consists in assessing whether the model's results correspond to the real world with regard to the reproduction of the 'stylised facts', especially if the main objective of the model is that of a conceptual experiment or to evaluate hypotheses or a theory, or of the 'real-world data', if the objective of the model is predictive. In every case, the 'empirical output validation' aim is to estimate if and how the stylised facts or the real data can belong to the outputs of the model. To such an aim, it can also be considered the 'cross-validation' that consists in estimating how much the results of the model in way of validation depart from those of a model already validated.

4. The 'parameterisation is the conformation with respect to correctness', namely, the quantification of parameters to make the results as close as possible to reality. A model is 'well parametrised' when the values of the parameters make it possible to interpret time series or real data or can replicate stylised facts. To this end, after verification and control have passed the test, falsification and parametrization can be reiterated. This means that once the consistency of the model has been ascertained, then various degrees of correctness can be reached repeating some passages of falsification, based on initial parameterizations, and of parameterization, to make the results increasingly approach the reality.

In this phase they can be lead of the 'test cases' said 'relative value test' with which it is checked if the relations noted between input and output change in a predictable way whenever some inputs are modified. At last, the 'empirical input validation' consists in estimating if the data that come supplied in input to the model are accurate and correspond to the reality represented from the model, in fact it is sufficient to describe like these data in input have been produced.

In the context of parameterization, estimation and calibration are adopted: some (e.g., Platt, 2020) find the distinction between these two terms unclear to the extent of not finding sufficient reasons to distinguish them, while others (Grazzini and Richiardi, 2015; Delli Gatti et al., 2018) distinguish between estimation and calibration. In any case, it is only after setting parameter values that we can proceed to run a simulation and compare the results with the reality of the data. A verified, controlled, falsified, and well parameterized model has reached the level of valid scientific knowledge base.

The calibration of an ABM is carried out to achieve results that are as close as possible to real data or known information, either empirically or automatically. Empirical calibration consists of conducting a controlled experiment to deduce the values of certain parameters from its outcome, or secondary data from similar experiments can be used. Within the framework of empirical calibration, one can also define the initial conditions of the quantities characterising the agents. Empirical calibration is based on real data, so it seems to be the preferable one because it is able to give a justification to the choice of parameters, but it has some drawbacks because it is very expensive – rewarding individuals, recruiting them, preparation and execution time – and it does not guarantee that the evolution of the model is valid because some parameters of the model could vary in time instead of being constant.[25] Automatic calibration is based on the use of calibration tools, such as 'genetic algorithms' or 'machine learning' procedures. Typically, automatic calibration considers a real training database, often smaller than the test database used for validation purposes. The former is used to identify the values of a set of parameters that make the simulated database as close as possible to the real training database. For example, employing the genetic algorithms, one specifies a 'fitness function' that must be optimised, usually minimised, with respect to a margin of error between simulated and real data: once the fitness function is established, the parametric setup that has generated the least error is adopted. The advantage of this practice is that it is managed by the computer, also using applications specifically designed for this purpose, so it is therefore particularly efficient and low-cost, but it has the disadvantage of leaving the choice of which measure to optimise to the researcher.[26] Sometimes more than one measure is used for different purposes, with the ex post evaluation of which solution is preferable. In addition, the correlation criterion can also be used to assess the best parameterisation, thus choosing the set of parameters that makes the simulated data more positively correlated with the real data. Another disadvantage of this practice is that, if the real training database is not representative of the real test database, it may not be possible to validate the conformity of the model with reality, even though it has been calibrated with real data: the solution, in this case, can be found by starting from an overall real database, extracting from it a statistically representative sample as the training database and using the remaining part in the test phase. Finally, in contrast to empirical calibration, rather than a disadvantage, automatic calibration has the not insignificant limitation of returning a valid parameterisation without explaining why, leaving this burden to the researcher.

Like calibration, ABM estimation employs real data to make inferences about model parameters.[27] However, unlike calibration, estimation uses an inferential structure, with given statistical properties, and does not take place at the same time as the simulation but is based on one or more simulations characterised by their parameters. Put another way, calibration runs the model to search for parameter values, while estimation employs the simulation run with a given set of parameters, perhaps those resulting from the calibration to improve them: in this case the calibration may serve to narrow the value space for the parameters. Again, the strategy is to optimise the parametric setup so that the model is as close as possible to the actual data – in fact, the minimisation of an error measure is still considered. The estimation can be based either on point

---

[25] See Colasante (2017) and literature cited therein.
[26] See, for instance, www.behaviorsearch.org.
[27] See Richiardi (2018), Bargigli (2017), and the literature cited therein.

data (simulated minimum distance method) or, as a special case, on moment data (method of simulated moments) of the empirical distribution of the real data. In any case, the estimation procedure is bound by the statistical criteria of the inferential method and may conclude with a result which, although optimal with respect to these criteria, may not be satisfactory from a practical point of view. That is, it may happen that the parameter estimate satisfies the inferential criteria but with an unsatisfactory 'fitting' capacity: for example, the various p-values may well be adequate, but the goodness of fit is insufficient to rely on this parameterisation. Finally, to clarify the difference between calibration and estimation, in Grazzini and Richiardi (2015) it is explained that calibration has as its main purpose to find results that are consistent with the observed data while estimation is also concerned with producing accurate estimates of the parameters of the data generating process (DGP). If no real data is available, one can only proceed to manual fine-tuning in the perspective of simulating stylised facts known in the literature.

2.5 Sensitivity Analysis

Sensitivity and uncertainty analysis of a mathematical simulation model that is run on a computer are the practices to be followed to 'study' the model so that it can be used consciously, which is especially relevant if the model is designed as a 'problem solving' or 'decision making' tool. These areas of research are constantly evolving, mainly due to the increasing computational capacity that makes them applicable to large-scale and complex models with many inputs such as parameters, assumptions, and exogenous data. The basic principle of sensitivity analysis is to assess the relative importance of the inputs to a model in terms of the variability of the outputs and in this respect it differs from uncertainty analysis, which is concerned with measuring how variable the predictions of a model are as the inputs change without assessing their relative importance. The two fields are distinct but are often confused as equivalent: 'This is perhaps due to an influential econometric paper (Leamer, 1985) . . . whose problem setting and motivation were to ensure the robustness of a regression analysis with respect to various modelling choices . . .. As a result, in economics and finance, it is common to see the expression "sensitivity analysis" used to mean . . . "uncertainty analysis"' (Saltelli et al., 2019; Learner, 1985). These authors then point out several problematic arguments of sensitivity and uncertainty analysis in many research fields, among these arguments the misinterpretation of terms and the different degree of statistical expertise are the most relevant. Above all, however, these authors emphasise the fact that sensitivity analysis and uncertainty do not have a circumscribed disciplinary scope because mathematical modelling is not a discipline in the proper sense.

As Morton and Tejada (2013) explain, in very general terms, sensitivity analysis of a model consists of varying some inputs, sometimes simultaneously, to evaluate the corresponding changes in the outputs. If we vary one input at a time (one-at-a-time; OAT), we speak of local methods. The OAT method is the simplest, and computationally least intensive, and consists of changing only one parameter while leaving all others unchanged to evaluate the effect of the variations, typically by considering the variance of the output. The merit of this method is that it allows one to easily trace the variations of the outputs that are more significant than those of the inputs that generated them. The limitation of this method is that when the model is very complex, inaccurate results may be obtained, also because the choice of which input to vary, and to what extent, is sometimes arbitrary. Moreover, since it only considers one input at a time, OAT does not allow for the evaluation of interactions between variations in the inputs.

Global methods allow the variation of several inputs together. For more complex models, sensitivity analysis is based on variance-based methods, such as Sobol (2001). This method estimates the contribution of each input to the model's uncertainty measure by means of two elements: the first-order sensitivity, which evaluates the contribution to the variance of the output for each input relative to the total variance, and the total sensitivity index, which evaluates the contribution to the variance of the output considering the uncertainty due to the interaction of the input with all others. The logic of this method is very simple but suffers from the fact that it assumes independence between all parameters, thus it does not allow for the evaluation of joint variance effects (Granato and Li-Jessen, 2020).

About sensitivity and uncertainty analysis, among others, the most important references are Saltelli et al. (2004), Saltelli et al. (2008), and Ghanem et al. (2017).

The basic idea of sensitivity analysis is very simple, but some terminological precautions are necessary. First, one must consider that by model inputs one means the parameters characterising the model variables, the functions describing them, or even the assumptions or hypotheses underlying the model specification. Secondly, one must consider that by outputs one does not mean the simulation results but the reliability measures that inform the correctness or fidelity of the underlying model with respect to the reality being modelled (Morton and Tejada, 2013). Dependent on these assumptions is the fact that outputs are always estimates derived from Monte Carlo sampling methods on the space of inputs and, therefore, output measures, in turn, are 'estimates', hence contain errors with respect to 'true values' that cannot in fact be calculated with absolute precision. The main sources of these errors are typically three: (i) those due to sampling on the parameter space, (ii) those due to uncertainties related to the inputs, and (iii) those due to the degree of correctness with which the underlying model represents reality.

There are several methods to sensitivity analysis, but all explore differences in outputs from changes in inputs. Depending on the method of changing the inputs and descriptively summarising the outputs, there may be different approaches to sensitivity analysis. However, regardless of the approach to sensitivity analysis, a key aspect is to understand which inputs are significant, that is, those that induce the most relevant changes in the outputs. This is particularly relevant when subjecting a model for 'problem-solving' or 'decision-making' to sensitivity analysis. In other words, we can consider sensitivity analysis as the phase of studying the model to identify the most 'sensitive' parts, so as to be able to control its behaviour and correct its weaknesses.

Among the most accredited practices for sensitivity analysis, Morton and Tejada (2013) propose a ten-step set of guidelines, which we merely list here, referring to their text for more details:

1. Define the sensitivity analysis model.
2. Select the outputs of interest.
3. Select the inputs of interest.
4. Select parameter values or their variation ranges.
5. Estimate outputs conditional on inputs.
6. Synthesise the outcome of the analysis using tornado-plots.
7. Quantify uncertainty graphically.
8. Synthesise input and output variations using spider-plots.
9. Visualise the simultaneous interaction of variations on multiple inputs.
10. Metamodels and experimental designs.

Saltelli et al. (2019) propose a list of best practices for conducting an adequate sensitivity analysis. First, they propose the global exploration of the input space, especially useful for models in which inputs interact with each other or in which many nonlinearities are found. Secondly, they propose conducting uncertainty analysis first to assess robustness and then sensitivity analysis to understand the major causes of variability. As a third piece of advice, they propose to focus the sensitivity and uncertainty analysis on one or a few precise questions because, typically, models have many outputs that can be used for different purposes, so the relationships between the inputs and the individual outputs may be different; therefore 'it is essential to focus the sensitivity analysis on the question addressed by the model rather than more generally on the model'. A fourth aspect considered important is 'reporting', that is, the need to infer the relative importance of inputs, and combinations thereof, through appropriate graphical methods and measurements. Finally, they point out that even the most rigorous sensitivity and uncertainty analyses do not guarantee the absence of errors because if the correctness of the model is poor, that is, if it is not a good representation of reality, measuring the sensitivity of a parameter is of little relevance.

In the more specific area of ABM models, ten Broecke et al. (2016) explain that even the most accredited sensitivity analysis methodologies may not be sufficient for an accurate analysis of ABM models precisely because of their specificities such as multi-level structures, interactions, nonlinearities, emergent phenomena, and self-organisation. These elements make it very difficult to link input and output as proposed by classical methods because it is a question of analysing complex adaptive systems. However, for an ABM to be usable for practical purposes, it is essential to understand the effects of different configurations on the overall results emerging from the system. The authors, through a comparative study of several methodologies, focus on three objectives of sensitivity analysis for ABMS: (i) to understand how emergent properties are generated by the ABM, (ii) to examine the robustness of the emergent properties and (iii) to quantify the variability of the results according to the parameters.

Borgonovo et al. (2022) propose a systematic approach for the sensitivity analysis of ABMS focusing on four purposes: (i) to assess the robustness of the results, (ii) to identify the elements with the greatest impact on the results, (iii) to understand how these elements interact, and (iv) in which direction the results vary as the identified elements vary. The authors define a general conceptual scheme to identify what they call 'moving parts', that is, the model components that can be varied to assess the model's sensitivity: parameters and procedures. Furthermore, an important contribution is to propose a variant of the individual conditional expectation (ICE) plots to take into account the stochastic nature of ABMS (S-ICE plot). The protocol proposed in this contribution consists of six steps, which we list here, referring to the text for further details:

1. Choose the outputs of interest,
2. Identify the objectives of the sensitivity analysis: prioritisation, direction of change, interaction quantification, robustness analysis,
3. Identify which elements of the model must vary,
4. Choose the appropriate sensitivity analysis method for target-element matching,
5. Evaluate parameters with reference values to build the baseline scenario (local analysis) or identifying ranges of variation (global analysis),
6. Summary and visualisation of results according to objective.

3 Conclusion

This Element is complementary to *Complexity in Economics* (Landini et al., 2024), where inconsistencies of mainstream economics have been discussed that can be overcome in the frame of Complexity Economics (Arthur, 2021; Rosser, 2021). There, we reinforced the purpose of the ABM simulation approach as the main tool for studying socioeconomic complex systems, as well as for specifying and implementing more general and realistic models. In this Element, we propose an overall and non-technical presentation of the main topics in ABM simulation. In Section 1 foundational notions are introduced with some historical background. Section 2 presents the general characteristics and tools of ABM with attention to advanced topics like validation and sensitivity analysis. The structure of the Element's sections includes a reasoned and selected set of bibliographical references.

The existence of competition between hierarchical economic institutions implies problems of computational complexity, which can be handled by the ABM method. This is an increasingly widely adopted approach, which differs from important precursors of computer simulation such as system dynamics, cellular automata, and microsimulation. Unlike ABM, system dynamics does not allow for the modelling of heterogeneous micro aspects, but only interdependencies and feedbacks between macro variables; cellular automata reduce the interaction of dispersed micro entities to a single homogeneous parameter; while microsimulation does not include interaction.[28]

Also, as Landini et al. (2024) highlight, Hahn shows that the AD model, being an axiomatic system, has no normative value – without even mentioning the SMD 'theorem'. Solow and Hanh (1997) then argue that reducing economic analysis to mathematical reasoning alone, as the Dynamic Stochastic General Equilibrium (DSGE) does, does not make economic sense. Instead, ABM manages to analyse the system of interrelationships between agents at several hierarchical levels through the analysis of nodes and the study of the topology of networks.

With ABM the methodology is 'bottom-up': individual parameters are estimated with experiments and econometric surveys, their statistical robustness – such as distribution – is assessed at an intermediate level between the micro and the macro, and finally it is evaluated whether aggregate regularities emerge in the whole. In short, there is micro, meso, and macro empirical validation and new economic policy applications and tools for both the meso sector level and the networks with which interactions can be analysed. The difference between microeconomics and macroeconomics is that the latter is the emergent result of the interaction and behaviour of agents at the micro level.

---

[28] Brancaccio et al. (2021) show that the ABM literature itself is not heterodox.

The ABM approach is growing fast and evidences of applicability and results about representation of real-world phenomena are accumulating. What is still missing is a unifying formal theory. Literature evolves fast to such an extent that it appears an 'uncultivated forest', hence there is need of systematisation. In economics, this is due to the fact that many scholars recognise the potentialities and advantages of ABM such that they prefer investing resources in the development of models to overcome dissatisfaction with the mainstream approach in economics. This blossoming without a formal theory does not come without consequences. For instance, many scholars are sceptical and think that ABM is a practice without theory, something far from an autonomous discipline, just like econometrics, that finds application in a wide spectrum of research fields.

Along this direction of theoretical research there is a lot of work that is to be done. In this Element, we hope to have at least posed the problem to stimulate students and scholars, mainly those that are not already familiar with this approach, to join the effort in the development of a formal ABM theory to upgrade the ABM approach to the status of a discipline with more defined boundaries.

List of Acronyms

ABM	Agent-Based Model, Modelling
ABMS	Agent-Based Model Simulation
ACE	Agent-Based Computational Economics
AD	Arrow-Debreu
AOP	Agent-Oriented Programming
API	Application Programming Interface
BDI	Beliefs-Desires-Intentions
CAS	Complex Adaptive System
DGP	Data Generating Process
DSGE	Dynamic Stochastic General Equilibrium
FIPA	Foundation for Intelligent Physical Agents
HPC	High Performance Computing
IDE	Integrated Development Environments
IEEE	Institute of Electrical and Electronics Engineers
OOP	Object Oriented Programming
SFC	Stock-Flow Consistent
SMD	Sonnenschein–Mantel–Debreu

References

Abar, S., Theodoropoulos, G. K., Lemarinier, P., and O'Hare, G. M., (2017), Agent Based Modelling and Simulation Tools: A Review of the State-of-Art Software, *Computer Science Review*, 24: 13–33.

Allan, R. J., (2010), Survey of Agent Based Modelling and Simulation Tools (Technical report, ISSN 1362-0207), Science & Technology Facilities Council, https://epubs.stfc.ac.uk/manifestation/5601/DLTR-2010-007.pdf.

Arrow, K. J., and Debreu, G., (1954), Existence of an Equilibrium for a Competitive Economy, *Econometrica*, 22(3): 265–290.

Arthur, W. B., (2021), Foundations of Complexity Economics, *Nature Reviews Physics*, 3: 136–145.

Assenza, T., and Delli Gatti, D., (2013), E Pluribus Unum: Macroeconomic Modelling for Multi-agent Economies, *Journal of Economic Dynamics and Control*, 37(8): 1659–1682.

Assenza, T., Delli Gatti, D., and Grazzini, J., (2015), Emergent Dynamics of a Macroeconomic Agent-Based Model with Capital and Credit, *Journal of Economic Dynamics and Control*, 50(C): 5–28.

Axelrod, R., (1997), *The Complexity of Cooperation: Agent-Based Models of Competition and Collaboration*, Princeton University Press.

Axtell, R. L., and Farmer, J. (2023), Agent-Based Modelling in Economics and Finance: Past, Present and Future, *Journal of Economic Literature*. www.aeaweb.org/articles?id=10.1257/jel.20221319&from=f.

Bădică, C., Budimac, Z., Burkhard, H. D., and Ivanović, M. (2011). Software Agents: Languages, Tools, Platforms, *Computer Science and Information Systems*, 8(2): 255–298.

Bak, P., Paczuski, M., and Shubik, M., (1996), Price Variations in a Stock Market with Many Agents, *Physica A: Statistical Mechanics and its Applications*, 246(3–4): 430–453.

Ballot, G., Mandel, A., and Vignes, A., (2015), Agent-Based Modeling and Economic Theory: Where Do We Stand?, Introduction to the Special Issue of the 17th WEHIA Conference, *Journal of Economic Interaction and Coordination*, 10: 199–220.

Bargigli, L., (2017), Econometric Methods or Agent-Based Model, in Gallegati, M., Palestrini, A., and Russo, A., et al., (eds.), *Introduction to Agent-Based Economics*, Academic Press: 163–189.

Bellomo, N., Bingham, R., Chaplain, M. A. J., Dosi, G., Forni, G., Knopoff, D. A., Lowengrub, J., Twarock, R. and Virgillito, M. E., (2020),

A Multiscale Model of Virus Pandemic: Heterogeneous Interactive Entities in a Globally Connected World, *Mathematical Models and Methods in Applied Sciences*, 30(8): 1591–1651.

Bergmann, B., (1974), A Microsimulation of the Macroeconomy with Explicitly Represented Money Flows, *Annals of Economic and Social Measurement*, 3(3): 475–479.

Bianchi, C., Cirillo, P., Gallegati, M., and Vagliasindi, P. A., (2008), Validation in Agent-Based Models: An Investigation on the CATS Model, *Journal of Economic Behavior and Organization*, 67(3–4): 947–964.

Billari, F. C., Fent, T., Prskawetz, A., and Scheffran, J., (2006), *Agent-Based Computational Modelling: An Introduction*, in Billari, F. C., Fent, T., Prskawetz, A., and Scheffran, J. (eds.), *Agent-Based Computational Modelling: Applications in Demography, Social, Economic and Environmental Sciences*, Physica: 1–16.

Bonabeau, E., (2002), Agent-Based Modeling: Methods and Techniques for Simulating Human Systems, *PNAS*, 99(3): 7280–7287.

Bookstaber, R., (2017), *The End of Theory: Financial Crises, the Failure of Economics, and the Sweep of Human Interaction*, Princeton University Press.

Bookstaber, R., and Kirman, A. P., (2018), Modeling a Heterogeneous World, in Hommes, C., and LeBaron, J., (eds.), *Handbook of Computational Economics*, Vol. 4, Chp. 14, pp. 769–795, Elsevier.

Bordini, R., Braubach, L., Dastani, M., Seghrouchni, A., Gomez-Sanz, J., Leite, J., O'Hare, G., Pokahr, A., and Ricci, A. (2006). A Survey of Programming Languages and Platforms for Multi-Agent Systems, *Informatica*, 30: 33–44.

Borgonovo, E., Pangallo, M., Rivkin, J., Rizzo, L., and Siggelkow, N., (2022), Sensitivity Analysis of Agent-Based Models: A New Protocol, *Computational and Mathematical Organization Theory*; DOI: https://doi.org/10.1007/s10588-021-09358-5.

Borrill, P. L., and Tesfatsion, L., (2010), *Agent-Based Modeling: The Right Mathematics of the Social Sciences?*, WP 10023, Iowa State University.

Brancaccio, E., Gallegati, M., and Giammetti, R., (2021), Neoclassical Influences in Agent-Based Literature: A Systematic Review, *Journal of Economic Surveys*, 36: 350–385.

Bratman, M. E., (1987), *Intention, Plans and Practical Reason*, Harvard University Press.

Caiani, A., and Caverzasi, E. (2017), *Decentralized Interacting Macroeconomcs and the Agent-Based 'Modellaccio'*, in Gallegati, M., Palestrini, A., and Russo, A., (eds.), *Introduction to Agent-Based Economics*, Academic Press: 15–64.

Caiani, A., Godin, A., Caverzasi, E., Gallegati, M., Kinsella, S., and Stiglitz, J. E., (2016), Agent-Based Stock-Flow Consistent Macroeconomics: Towards a Benchmark Model, *Journal of Economic Dynamics and Control*, 69: 375–408.

Caldarelli, G. (2010), *Complex Networks*, UNESCO-EOLSS. www.eolss.net/ebooklib/bookinfo/complex-networks.aspx.

Caldarelli, G., and Catanzaro, M., (2012), *Networks: A Very Short Introduction*, Oxford University Press.

Caldarelli, G., and Chesa, A., (2016), *Data Science and Complex Networks: Real Case Studies with Python*, Oxford University Press.

Casti, J., (1979), *Connectivity, Complexity and Catastrophes in Large-Scale Systems*, John Wiley & Sons.

Cincotti, S., Raberto, M., and Teglio, A., (2010), Credit Money and Macroeconomic Instability in the Agent-Based Model and Simulator Economics, *Economics: The Open Access, Open Assessment E-Journal*, 4. www.economics-ejournal.org/economics/discussionpapers/2010-4.

Cincotti, S., Raberto, M., and Teglio, A., (2012), The EURACE Macroeconomics Model and Simulator, in *Agent-based Dynamics, Norms, and Corporate Governance*, The Proceedings of the 16th World Congress of the International Economic Association, Palgrave Macmillan.

Cioffi-Revilla, C., (2017), *Introduction to Computational Social Science: Principles and Applications*, Springer.

Colasante, A., (2017), *Experimental Economics for ABM Validation*, in Gallegati, M., Palestrini, A., and Russo, A., et al., (eds.), *Introduction to Agent-Based Economics*, Academic Press.

Dawid, H., Gemkow, S., Harting, P., van der Hoog, S., and Neugart, M., (2018), *Agent-Based Macroeconomic Modeling and Policy Analysis: The Eurace@Unibi Model*, in Chen, S.-H., Kaboudan, M., Du, Y.-R., (eds.), *The Oxford Handbook of Computational Economics and Finance*, Oxford University Press: 490–519.

Delli Gatti, D., Desiderio, S., Gaffeo, E., Cirillo, P., and Gallegati, M., (2011), *Macroeconomics From the Bottom-Up*, Springer.

Delli Gatti, D., Di Guilmi, C., Gaffeo, E., Giulioni, G., Gallegati, M., and Palestrini, A., (2005), A New Approach to Business Fluctuations: Heterogeneous Interacting Agents, Scaling Laws and Financial Fragility, *Journal of Economic Behavior and Organization*, 56(4): 489–512.

Delli Gatti, D., Fagiolo, G., Gallegati, M., Richiardi, M., and Russo, A., (2018), *Agent-Based Models in Economics: A Toolkit*, Cambridge University Press.

Delli Gatti D., Gaffeo, E., and Gallegati, M., (2010). Complex Agent-Based Macroeconomics: A Manifesto for a New Paradigm, *Journal of Economic Interaction and Coordination*, 5(2): 111–135.

Delli Gatti, D., Gaffeo, E., Gallegati, M., Giulioni, G., Kirman, A. P., Palestrini, A., and Russo, A., (2007), Complexity Dynamics and Empirical Evidence, *Information Science*, 177(5): 1204–1221.

Di Guilmi, C., Landini, S., and Gallegati, M., (2017), *Interactive Macroeconomics: Stochastic Aggregate Dynamics with Heterogeneous and Interacting Agents*, Cambridge University Press.

Dosi, G. (2023). *The Foundations of Complex Evolving Economies*. Oxford University Press.

Dosi, G., Fagiolo, G., and Roventini, A., (2010), Schumpeter Meeting Keynes: A Policy-Friendly Model of Endogenous Growth and Business Cycle, *Journal of Economic Dynamics and Control*, 34(9): 1748–1767.

Dosi, G., Fagiolo, G., Napoletano, M., and Roventini, A., (2013), Income Distribution, Credit and Fiscal Policies in an Agent-Based Keynesian Model, *Journal of Economic Dynamics and Control*, 37(8): 1598–1625.

Epstein, J. M., and Axtell, R. L., (1996), *Growing Artificial Societies: Social Science from the Bottom Up*. Massachusetts Institute of Technology Press.

Fagiolo, G., and Richiardi, M., (2018), *Empirical Validation of Agent-Based Models*, in Delli Gatti, D., Fagiolo, G., Gallegati, M., Richiardi, M., and Russo, A., (eds.), *Agent-Based Models in Economics: A Toolkit*, Cambridge University Press.

Farmer, D. J., and Foley, D. K., (2009), The Economy Needs Agent-Based Modeling, *Nature*, 460(7256): 685–686.

Frank, U., Squazzoni, F., and Troitzsch, K. G., (2009), *EPOS-Epistemological Perspectives on Simulation: An Introduction*, in Squazzoni, F. (ed.), *Epistemological Aspects of Computer Simulation in the Social Sciences*. EPOS 2006. Lecture Notes in Computer Science, vol. 5466. Springer. DOI: https://doi.org/10.1007/978-3-642-01109-2_1.

Friedman, M., (1953), *Essays in Positive Economics*, University of Chicago Press.

Gallegati, M., and Kirman, A. P., (2019), 20 Years of WEHIA: A Journey in Search of a Safer Road, *Journal of Economic Behavior and Organization*, 157(C): 5–14.

Gardner, M., (1970), The Fantastic Combinations of John Conway's New Solitaire Game 'life', Mathematical Games, *Scientific American*, 223(4): 120–123.

Ghanem, M., Higdon, D., and Owhadi, H., (2017), *Handbook of Uncertainty Quantification*, Springer.

Gilbert, N., (2020), *Agent-Based Models*, SAGE Publications Series, n. 153,

Gilbert, N., and Troitzsch, K. G., (1999), *Simulation for the Social Scientist*, Open University Press.

Giordano, G., Blanchini, F., Bruno, R., Colaneri, P., Di Filippo, A., Di Matteo, A., and Colaneri, M., (2020), Modelling the COVID-19 Epidemic and Implementation of Population-wide Interventions in Italy, *Nature Medicine Letters*, www.nature.com/articles/s41591-020-0883-7.

Granato, B., and Li-Jessen, N. Y. K., (2020), Sensitivity Analysis for Dimensionality Reduction in Agent-Based Modeling, Proceedings of the 24th European Conference on AI – ECAI 2020 At: Santiago de Compostela, Spain. https://ecai2020.eu/papers/1396_paper.pdf.

Grazzini, J., and Richiardi, M., (2015), Estimation of Agent-Based Models by Simulated Minimum Distance, *Journal of Economic Dynamics and Control*, 51: 148–165.

Greenblat, C. S., (1971), Simulation, Games, and the Sociologist, *The American Sociologist*, 6: 161–164.

Hamil, L., and Gilbert, N., (2016), *Agent-Based Modelling in Economics*, John Wiley & Sons, Ltd.

Holland, J., and Miller, J. H., (1991), Artificial Adaptive Agents in Economic Theory, *The American Economic Review*, Papers and Proceedings of the Hundred and Third Annual Meeting of the American Economic Association (May), 81(2): 365–370.

Hommes, C., (2013), *Behavioral Rationality and Heterogeneous Expectations in Complex Economic Systems*, Cambridge University Press.

Hommes, C., Poledna, S., and Zahng, Y., (2021), *Next-Generation Agent-Based Model of Canada* (CAN-ABM). www.bankofcanada.ca/wp-content/uploads/2021/11/agent-based-model-canada-yang-zhang.pdf.

Ioannides, Y. M. (1990), Trading Uncertainty and Market Form, *International Economic Review*, 31(3): 619–638.

Jacobs, B. I., Levy, K. N., and Markowitz, H. M., (2004), Financial Market Simulation. *Journal of Portfolio Management*, 30th Anniversary Issue: 142–151.

Kim, G., and Markowitz, H. M., (1989), Investment Rules, Margin and Market Volatility, *Journal of Portfolio Management*, 16(1): 45–52.

Kirman, A. P., (1983), Communication in Markets: A Suggested Approach, *Economics Letters*, 12: 1–5.

Kirman A. P., (1999), Interaction and Markets, in Gallegati, M., and Kirman, A. P., (eds.), *Beyond the Representative Agent*, Edward Elgar.

Kirman, A. P., Oddou, C., and Weber, S., (1986), Stochastic Communication and Coalition Formation, *Econometrica*, 54: 129–138.

Knoke, D., and Yang, S. (2019), *Social Network Analysis*, SAGE Publications.

Kravari, K., and Bassiliades, N. (2015). A Survey of Agent Platforms, *Journal of Artificial Societies and Social Simulation*, 18(1): 11, http://jasss.soc.surrey.ac.uk/18/1/11.html, DOI: https://doi.org/10.18564/jasss.2661.

Krešimir, R., Rosić, M., and Boljat, I., (2020) A Survey of Agent-Based Modelling and Simulation Tools for Educational Purpose, *Technical Gazette* 27, 3(2020): 1014–1020; retrieved January 2022 from https://hrcak.srce.hr/file/347094.

Landini, S., and Gallegati, M., (2014), Heterogeneity, Interaction and Emergence: Effects of Composition, *International Journal of Computational Economics and Econometrics*, 4(3/4): 339–361.

Landini, S., Gallegati, G., and Gallegati, M., (2024), *Complexity in Economics*, Cambridge Elements in Complexity and Agent-based Economics, Cambridge University Press.

Landini, S., Gallegati, M., and Rosser, B. Jr, (2020) Consistency and Incompleteness in General Equilibrium Theory, *Journal of Evolutionary Economics*, 30: 205–230.

Landini, S., Gallegati, M., and Stiglitz, J. E., (2015), Economies with Heterogeneous Interacting Learning Agents, *Journal of Economic Interaction and Coordination*, 10(1): 91–118; 13.

Landini, S., Gallegati, M., Stiglitz, J. E., Xhiao, L., and Di Guilmi, C., (2014), Learning and Macroeconomic Dynamics, in Dieci, R., He, T., and Hommes, C., (eds.), *Advances in Nonlinear Economic Dynamics and Quantitative Finance, Essays in Honour of Carl Chiarella*, Springer: 109–134.

Langton, C., (1995), *Artificial Life: An Overview*. Massachusetts Institute of Technology Press.

Leamer, E. E., (1985), Sensitivity Analyses Would Help, *The American Economic Review*, 75(3): 308–313.

LeBaron, B., and Tesfatsion, L., (2008), Modeling Macroeconomies as Open-Ended Dynamic Systems of Interacting Agents, *American Economic Review*, 98(2): 246–250.

Leon, F., Paprzycki, M., and Ganzha, M. (2015). *A Review of Agent Platforms*. Technical Report, MultiParadigm Modelling for Cyber-Physical Systems (MPM4CPS), ICT COST Action IC1404, 16 pages, updated June 2018, DOI: https://doi.org/10.13140/RG.2.2.32356.76167

Luke, S., Cioffi-Revilla, C., Panait, L., Sullivan, K., and Balan, G., (2005), MASON: A Multi-Agent Simulation Environment. *Simulation: Transactions of the Society for Modeling and Simulation International*, 82(7): 517–527.

Macal, C. M., (2004), *Agent-Based Modeling and Social Simulation with Mathematica and MATLAB*, in Proceedings of the Agent 2004 Conference on Social Dynamics: Interaction, Reflexivity and Emergence, ANL/DIS-05–6, C. M. Macal, D. Sallach, and M. J. North (eds.), co-sponsored by Argonne National Laboratory and The University of Chicago, October 7–9.

Minar, N., Burkat, R., Langton, G., and Sakenzi, M., (1996), *The Swarm Simulation System: A Toolkit for Building Multi-Agent Simulations*, Tech. Rep., WP96-06–042, Santa Fe Institute.

Morton, D., and Tejada, J., (2013), A Practical Guide to Sensitivity Analysis of a Large-Scale Computer Simulation Model, South Texas Project Risk-Informed GSI-191 Evaluation, https://jjtejada.files.wordpress.com/2014/01/sensitivity_analysis_with_appendix.pdf.

North, M. J., (2014), A Theoretical Formalism for Analyzing Agent-Based Models, *Complex Adaptive Systems*, 2: 3.

North, M. J., Collier, N. T., and Vos, J. R., (2006), Experiences Creating Three Implementations of the Repast Agent Modeling Toolkit, *ACM Transactions on Modeling and Computer Simulation*, 16(1): 1–25.

Orcutt, G. H., (1957), A New Type of Socio-Economic System, *The Review of Economics and Statistics*, 39(2): 116–123.

Pal, C. V., Leon, F., Paprzycki, M., and Ganzha, M., (2020), *A Review of Platforms for the Development of Agent Systems.* arXiv: https://arxiv.org/ftp/arxiv/papers/2007/2007.08961.pdf.

Palestrini, A., Gallegati, M., and Delli Gatti, D., (2021), *Adaptive Agents May Be Smarter Than You Think: Unbiasedness in Adaptive Expectations*, CESifo Working Paper No. 9205.

Parisi, G., (2006), *La Chiave, la Luce e l'Ubriaco*, Di Renzo Editore; second edition, 2021.

Pescarmona, G., Terna, P., Acquadro, A., Pescarmona, P., Russo, G., and Terna, S. (2020), *How Can ABM Models Become Part of the Policy-Making Process in Times of Emergencies: The S.I.S.A.R. Epidemic Model*, https://rofasss.org/2020/10/20/sisar/.

Platt, D., (2020), A Comparison of Economic Agent-Based Model Calibration Methods, *Journal of Economic Dynamic and Control*, 113(C): 103859.

Poledna, S., Miess, M. G., and Hommes, C. H., (2020), *Economic Forecasting with an Agent-Based Model* (February 24, 2020). SSRN: https://ssrn.com/abstract=3484768 or http://dx.doi.org/10.2139/ssrn.3484768.

Railsback, S. F, and Grimm, V., (2019), *Agent-Based and Individual-Based Modeling: A Practical Introduction*, Princeton University Press.

Rand, W., and Rust, R. T., (2011), Agent-Based Modelling in Marketing: Guidelines of Rigor, *International Journal of Research in Marketing*, 28(3): 181–193.

Reichardt, J., (2009), *Structures in Complex Networks*, Springer.

Reynolds, C. W., (1987), Flocks, Herds, and Schools: A Distributed Behavioral Model, *ACM SIGGRAPH Computer Graphics*, 21(4): 25–34.

Riccetti, L., Russo, A., and Gallegati, M., (2015), An Agent Based Decentralized Matching Macroeconomic Model, *Journal of Economic Interaction and Coordination*, 10(2): 305–332.

Richiardi, M., (2018), *Estimation of Agent-Based Models*, in Delli Gatti, D., Fagiolo, G., Gallegati, M., Richiardi, M., and Russo, A., (eds.), *Agent-Based Models in Economics. A Toolkit*, Cambridge University Press.

Rosen, R., (1985), *Anticipatory Systems: Philosophical, Mathematical and Methodological Foundations*, Pergamon Press.

Rosen, R., (1986), *On Information and Complexity*, in Casti, J. L., and Kerlqvist, A., (eds.), *Complexity, Mathematics and Life: Mathematical Approaches, Biomathematics*, Vol. 16. DOI: https://doi.org/10.1007/978-3-642-70953-1_7.

Rosser, J. B., Jr., (2021), *Foundations and Applications of Complexity Economics*, Springer Nature Switzerland.

Russo, A., Riccetti, L., and Gallegati, M., (2016), Increasing Inequality, Consumer Credit and Financial Fragility in an Agent Based Macroeconomic Model, *Journal of Evolutionary Economics*, 26(1): 25–47.

Saltelli, A., Aleksankina, K., Becker, W., Fennell, P., Ferretti, F., Holst, N., Li, S., and Wu, Q., (2019), Why so many published sensitivity analyses are false: A systematic review of sensitivity analysis practices, *Environmental Modelling & Software*, 114: 29–39.

Saltelli, A., Ratto, M., Andres, T., Campolongo, F., Cariboni, J., Gatelli, D., Saisana, M., and Tarantola, S., (2008), *Global Sensitivity Analysis: The Premier*, Wiley-Interscience.

Saltelli, A., Tarantola, S., Campolongo, F., and Ratto, M., (2004), *Sensitivity Analysis in Practice: A Guide to Assessing Scientific Models*, John Wiley and Sons.

Sargent, T., (1993), *Bounded Rationality in Macroeconomics*, Oxford University Press.

Schelling, T. C., (1971), Dynamic Models of Segregation, *The Journal of Mathematical Sociology*, 1(2): 143–186.

Scott, J., and Carrington, P. J., (2011), *The SAGE Handbook of Social Network Analysis*, SAGE Publications.

Simon, H., (1957), *A Behavioral Model of Rational Choice, in Models of Man, Social and Rational: Mathematical Essays on Rational Human Behavior in a Social Setting*, Wiley.

Simon, H., (1963), *Testability and Approximation*, in Hausman, D., (ed.), *The Philosophy of Economics*, Cambridge University Press: 179–182.

Sobol, I. M., (2001), Global Sensitivity Indices for Nonlinear Mathematical Models and Their Monte Carlo Estimates, *Mathematics and Computers in Simulation*, 55(1–3): 271–280.

Solow, R., and Hanh, F., (1997), *A Critical Essay on Modern Macroeconomic Theory*, Massachusetts Institute of Technology Press.

Squazzoni, F., (2010), The Impact of Agent-Based Models in the Social Sciences: After 15 Years of Incursion, *History of Economic Ideas*, 18(2): 197–233.

Standish, R. K., and Leow, R. (2003), *EcoLab: Agent Based Modeling for C++ Programmers*, in Proceedings SwarmFest 2003. arXiv:cs.MA/0401026.

ten Broecke, G., van Voorn, G., and Ligtenberg, A., (2016), Which Sensitivity Analysis Method Should I Use for My Agent-Based Model? *Journal of Artificial Science and Social Simulation*, 19(1): 5; www.jasss.org/19/1/5.html.

Terna, P., (2019), *SLAPP (Swarm-Like Protocol in Python) Reference Handbook*; https://terna.github.io/SLAPP3/SLAPP_Reference_Handbook.pdf.

Tesfatsion, L., (2021), *Agent-Based Computational Economics: Overview and Brief History*; https://dr.lib.iastate.edu/entities/publication/0e69f7c9-ad39-45b1-bcd7-3ba2023d6192.

Tesfatsion, L., and Judd, K., (2006), *Handbook of Computational Economics: Agent-Based Computational Economics*: 2, North-Holland.

Turrell, A., (2013), *Agent-Based Models: Understanding the Economy from the Bottom Up*, Quarterly Bulletin 2016 Q4, Bank of England, https://www.bankofengland.co.uk/quarterly-bulletin/2016/q4/agent-based-models-understanding-the-economy-from-the-bottom-up.

von Neumann, J., (1951), *The General and Logical Theory of Automata*, in Jeffress, L. A., (ed.), *Cerebral Mechanisms in Behavior* – The Hixon Symposium, John Wiley & Sons, pp. 1–31.

Wasserman, S., and Faust, K., (2008), *Social Network Analysis: Methods and Applications*, Cambridge University Press.

Wilensky, U., and Rand, W., (2015), *An Introduction to Agent-Based Modeling: Modeling Natural, Social, and Engineered Complex Systems with NetLogo*, Massachusetts Institute of Technology Press.

Wilensky, U., (1999–2019), *Types of Agents in NetLogo, The Center for Connected Learning and Computer-Based Modeling (CCL)*. Northwestern University.

Windrum, P., Fagiolo, G., and Moneta, A., (2007), Empirical Validation of Agent-Based Models: Alternatives and Prospects, *Journal of Artificial Societies and Social Simulation*, 10(2): 8.

Acknowledgements

For all the comments and constructive criticism, we are indebted to Silvano Cincotti, Domenico Delli Gatti, Tiziana Di Matteo, Giovanni Dosi, Magda Fontana, Alan Kirman, Fabrizio Lillo, Valerio Lucarini, Rosario Mantegna, Salvatore Micciché, Luciano Pietronero, Flaminio Squazzoni, Francesco Sylos Labini and, in particular, to Robert Axtell, Pietro Terna and Leigh Tesfatstion.

Complexity and Agent-Based Economics

Giovanni Dosi

Sant'Anna School of Advanced Studies

Giovanni Dosi is Professor Emeritus of Economics at Sant'Anna School of Advanced Studies, Pisa (Italy) and Editor for the Americas of the journal *Industrial and Corporate Change*. He is included in the ISI Highly Cited Research list, denoting those who made fundamental contributions to the advancement of science and technology, and is a corresponding member of the Accademia Nazionale dei Lincei, the first academy of sciences in Italy. He received, in 2016, the Wiley TIM Distinguished Scholar Award by the Technology and Innovation Management Division of the American Academy of Management, in 2022 the Penrose Prize of the European Academy of Management, and, in 2024, the Schumpeter Prize. His major research areas – where he is author and editor of several works – include economics of innovation and technological change, industrial economics, evolutionary theory, economic growth and development, organizational studies.

Mauro Gallegati

Università Politecnica delle Marche, Ancona

Mauro Gallegati is full Professor of Advanced Economics at the Università Politecnica delle Marche, Ancona. His research concerns interdisciplinary applications of complex systems with heterogeneous interacting agents and econophysics. He is one of the pioneers of agent-based models and economic complexity. He published several papers and books. His methods of asymmetric information settings are widely used by academicians. His research interests range from ABM economics to economic history, to mathematics, to complexity and networks.

Simone Landini

IRES Piemonte, Torino

Simone Landini is Senior Researcher at the Socioeconomic Research Institute of Piedmont (IRES Piemonte), Turin, Italy. He holds a PhD in Mathematics for the Analysis of Financial Markets, had been awarded the INET Grant and had been a Visiting Fellow in the University of Technology of Sydney. His research interests include applied mathematics, quantitative methods for economics, finance, regional and social sciences, agent-based modelling and computability theory. He published articles in international peer-reviewed journals.

Maria Enrica Virgillito

Sant'Anna School of Advanced Studies

Maria Enrica Virgillito is Associate Professor in Economics at the Institute of Economics, Sant'Anna School of Advanced Studies, Pisa, Italy where she coordinates the Seasonal School in "Agent-Based models in Economics". Her publications have been hosted in a number of international scientific peer-reviewed journals in the realms of complexity economics, institutional labour economics, evolutionary economics. She is Global Labour Organization Fellow and serves as Editor for the Macro and Development yearly issue of *Industrial and Corporate Change*, as Associate Editor for *Structural Change and Economic Dynamics* and for the *Review of Evolutionary Political Economy*.

About the Series

Elements in Complexity and Agent-Based Economics will present the state-of-the-art in complexity and agent-based economics with the aim of offering a systematic and easy-to-access thematic organization of both consolidated results, and the latest developments in the fields. Contributions are meant both as a support to scholarly research and as teaching tools.

Cambridge Elements ≡

Complexity and Agent-Based Economics

Elements in the Series

Complexity in Economics
Simone Landini, Giacomo Gallegati and Mauro Gallegati

Active Particles Methods in Economics: New Perspectives in the Interaction between Mathematics and Economics
Nicola Bellomo, Diletta Burini, Valeria Secchini, and Pietro Terna

Agent-Based Modelling: A Tool for Complexity
Mauro Gallegati, Simone Landini and Giacomo Gallegati

A full series listing is available at: www.cambridge.org/ECAE

Printed in the United States
by Baker & Taylor Publisher Services